D. H. WILSON

# Living
# with
# Other People

T0204233

Kenneth R. Melchin

# Living
# with
# Other People

**An Introduction to Christian Ethics
Based on Bernard Lonergan**

Saint Paul University
Series in ethics

© 1998 Novalis, Saint Paul University, Ottawa

Published in Canada by Novalis and in the U.S.A. by The Liturgical Press.

Cover and layout: Christiane Lemire

Novalis
49 Front St. East, Second Floor
Toronto, Ontario
M5E 1B3
1-800-387-7164 or (416) 363-3303

The Liturgical Press
St. John's Abbey
P.O. Box 7500
Collegeville, MN 56321-7500
USA

ISBN 2-89088-755-3

ISBN 0-8146-5940-3

The Appendix, a Study Guide to the text, was written by Paul Allen and Peter Monette.

Grateful acknowledgement is made to Barmarick Publications and the editor of *Humanomics* for permission to reprint selected passages from "Economies, Ethics, and the Structure of Social Living," *Humanomics* 10 (1994): 21-57, by Kenneth R. Melchin, © Patrington Press.

Printed in Canada


Canadian Cataloguing-in-Publication Data

Melchin, Kenneth R., 1949-
Living with other people: an introduction
to Christian ethics based on Bernard Lonergan
(Saint Paul University series in ethics)
Includes bibliographical references and index.
ISBN 2-89088-755-3

1. Christian ethics.  2. Lonergan, Bernard J. F.
(Bernard Joseph Brancis), 1904-1984. I. Title.
II. Series.

BJ1249.M43  1998      241     C97-900711-9

NOVALIS

A Michael Glazier Book
THE LITURGICAL PRESS
Collegeville, Minnesota

THIS BOOK IS DEDICATED TO
SANDIE, DEREK, NICHOLAS,
AND PATRICK,
FROM WHOM
I HAVE LEARNED
ABOUT LIVING
WITH OTHER
PEOPLE.

# Contents

# Preface

This book has two objectives: (1) to present the main elements of a study of Christian ethics based on the work of Bernard Lonergan; and (2) to provide readers with basic tools for moral self-understanding and deliberation. My chief goal, throughout, is to make Lonergan's work on ethics accessible to the general public.

This is no easy task, however. Lonergan's writings are complex, and it would be a disservice to the reader to oversimplify his thought. After all, Lonergan's work is not a body of information; it is a strategy for understanding and taking responsibility for the operations of one's own conscious living. This is an activity that the reader must perform if he or she is to gain understanding.

I have taken the rather hazardous route of omitting an explicit discussion of Lonergan's work to allow the reader to focus on the relevant line of self-inquiry. For those interested in reading further, I have provided references to primary and secondary resources from Lonergan studies in the notes and bibliography. At a number of points I contrast Lonergan's approach with alternative ways of raising questions and wrestling with issues.

There is one further point: the range of insights introduced in this text is quite limited. Where Lonergan often moves from initial insights, through a range of conceptual differentiations, to higher viewpoints, all within sentences and paragraphs, I have devoted more time to illustrating the initial questions, clues, and insights to help readers grasp more clearly the line of analysis. My aim throughout has been to engage introductory readers in the inquiry without sacrificing the principal elements of Lonergan's work in ethics. If I am successful in this task, I am confident that the ample resources provided by my colleagues in Lonergan studies will help readers advance along the road of conceptual development and refinement.

Still, this book does require a certain amount of work on the reader's part. Lonergan's approach is quite unusual, and first-time readers often find the discrepancies between their anticipations and the inner logic of the analyses quite unsettling. Nonetheless, the rewards are worth the work, and breakthroughs to self-understanding can be anticipated.

The notes and bibliography are not exhaustive. My goal is to provide the introductory-level reader with an initial point of access to further literature on selected topics treated throughout the text. Wherever possible, I have cited dictionary articles written for the intelligent layperson.

I am grateful to all of my colleagues who took the trouble to read through drafts of chapters and provide helpful comments: James Pambrun, Barry Meyers, Richard Hardy, Barbara Bozak, and Normand Bonneau. Chris Humphrey of Novalis was extremely helpful in providing editorial advice and Christiane Lemire made her excellent artistic contribution to the cover and layout. I am especially grateful to Michael O'Hearn and Stephen Scharper of Novalis for their patience, encouragement, and thoughtful advice at every stage along the way. Needless to say, the responsibility for the final shape of the text, for better or for worse, is my own.

I owe a debt of gratitude to my colleagues in the Faculty of Theology at Saint Paul University, most particularly my fellow ethicists: Jean-Marc Larouche, Hubert Doucet, and Gregory Walters. Christian ethics is a vibrant, collaborative activity at Saint Paul and I worked out many of the ideas for this book in dialogue with them. Our former Dean and colleague, the late André Guindon, played a leading role in making this a profoundly sane and decent place to work. He is missed by all of us.

I am grateful for the support and intellectual enrichment provided by my friends and colleagues in the field of Lonergan studies, particularly those at the Lonergan Centres at Boston College and Regis College, Toronto. I owe my greatest debt to Sean McEvenue and Philip McShane for introducing me to Lonergan's work.

I would like to thank the students in the undergraduate and graduate programs in theology at Saint Paul University. This text was worked out over the course of fifteen years of teaching. I cannot begin to measure the debt I owe to their insights, their integrity, and their faith. I am privileged to work with such a fine group of women and men.

Last but by no means least, I thank my wife and children, to whom this book is dedicated. There is no experience of living with other people more intense than a family, and ours is for me a joy beyond measure.

Research for sections of Chapter 2 was carried out with the aid of a grant from the Social Sciences and Humanities Research Council of Canada, 1989–90.

# Introduction
# A Strategy for Moral Understanding

If the daily news is a reliable indicator, ethics has become a growth industry. A brief look at any day's news reveals a bewildering array of ethical issues arising in every field of life: conflict-of-interest issues in business; scandals in government; sexual harassment in the workplace; charges of misappropriation of public funds; women's rights; questions of justice in international trade agreements; unethical activities in the military; the rise in organized crime in Eastern Europe; ongoing debates over native rights; and the perennial clashes among interest groups over issues of environment, homosexuality, abortion, euthanasia, genetic engineering, pornography, health care, education, and the future of our social services. The list goes on and on.

To be sure, ethics is in the forefront of public attention. Yet while public attention to ethical problems seems at an all-time high, public agreement on how to approach the problems seems to have reached an all-time low. Disagreement in ethics is the order of the day. To make matters worse, people who agree on issues need only give reasons for their views and they invariably find themselves in hot debate with friends, allies, and colleagues. Debates over issues give rise to debates over theories, methods, principles, and approaches. Eventually, the very meanings of the words, *ethical, moral, right,* and *wrong* are called into question. Our inability to agree on the basics begins eroding our confidence in any efforts to tackle the problems.

We have mixed reactions to this situation. Many of us feel that this diversity of opinion should be normal in a democracy. Ethics, after all, is simply private opinion, and in democratic society, private life is a matter of the free choice of individual citizens. Your values are your beliefs, and the law protects freedom of belief against arbitrary intrusion by others.

Others think differently. For this group, ethics clearly has a dramatic effect on public life. The jumble of voices in ethics is neither normal nor healthy; it is a sign of the breakdown of society. The solution is to return to traditional moral rules. Modern culture and modern media, with their cult of greed and their lure of endless gratification, are the cause of the malaise. The restoration of traditional moral discipline is the only thing that can deliver us.

Still others are not so sure. Some of us remember the old days with a little too much clarity. We recall the violence, the oppression, the sexism, the racism, the elitism, the constraints on creativity, and the violations of rights that they carried with them. Perhaps an aggressive commitment to rights can provide the foundation for ethics.

When we are faced with the bewildering array of claims currently made in the name of rights, however, this approach starts losing its appeal. How do we settle conflicting rights claims? Every interest group promotes its own agenda in the name of rights. Conflicts among these groups are tearing us apart. Whose rights take priority? Are some rights more urgent, more justifiable, more moral than others?

Perhaps the source of the problem lies in our leadership. Have our leaders given in to special interest groups? Have they lost their nerve? Or maybe they are corrupt? Mediocrity and corruption at the top seem to be all too rampant. For some of us, good leadership is the foundation of an ethical society.

At this point, more radical voices often intervene. They argue that bad leaders are made by society itself. They are the products of "social structures" that oppress the weak, bolster the rich, and promote systemic inequalities. To change social structures, they argue, requires social action, protests, lobbying, perhaps civil disobedience. In the final analysis, only such forms of "revolutionary" activity will clean out the old order and clear the way for a truly moral society.

But to these voices, the lessons of modern history seem to offer contrary evidence. Have we not tried the leftist approaches and found them wanting? In Eastern Europe the communist regimes have all fallen. In our own societies, the decades of government programs designed to redress structural inequities have left us bankrupt, with no sign of reductions in the social ills they were meant to cure. Ethical responsibility in the current age, some argue, requires liberty, fiscal responsibility, freedom in the marketplace, and, above all, no government intervention.

Still, we remain unconvinced. Is this all there is to ethics, an endless bickering along simplistic lines? The array of conflicting voices leaves us utterly confused. Each diagnosis of the problem seems to marshal its handful of data in support of its claims. Too many pieces of the puzzle still seem to be missing.

To make matters worse, each view formulates its prescription as an urgent call to action that casts doubt on the moral integrity of anyone who disagrees. Even when arguments leave us unconvinced, the rhetoric of urgency and responsibility adds to our anxiety. The diversity of voices leaves us unwilling to commit ourselves, and they make us feel anxious and guilty about our lack of commitment. This is not fair! There is something wrong with the whole appeal to morals and ethics. It seems like a sham! We feel a strange and unsettling inclination to give up on ethics itself.

How are we to find our way through this mess? The diversity of diagnoses is as bewildering as the diversity of positions on the issues. In fact, they both seem to stem from a common problem: we have difficulty knowing what counts as reliable evidence in ethics; we do not seem to be able to distinguish reliable knowledge from counterfeit opinion; we do not know where to begin to understand the issues. We have lost confidence in our very ability to understand. What is understanding in ethics anyway? How does it work? Where does "ethical knowledge" come from?

## Understanding Moral Knowing: The Process of Self-Discovery

The discussions in the following chapters will explore this idea of "ethical knowledge." Instead of focussing on the results or products of our moral knowing, the moral prescriptions, rules, and formulations that we confront in our social experience, we will attend to the *process* of moral knowing itself. We will explore how it "works," how it affects the life of the person engaged in the process, where we can expect reliable lines of ethical inquiry to go forward, and what kind of "knowledge" we attain in moral knowing. Rather than proposing answers to specific ethical questions or evaluating alternative approaches, we will sketch the processes that lead to such answers and evaluations.

The approach to moral knowing that is developed here is rooted in the philosophy of Bernard Lonergan (1904–1984). Throughout I draw upon a range of primary and secondary texts from the field of Lonergan studies and cite many of these texts in the notes and bibliography.[1] Lonergan's work, however, does not aim at providing you, the reader, with cold logic or authoritative argument about moral life. Rather, it is an invitation for you to embark upon a fascinating journey of self-discovery. We all live our daily lives engaged in acts of moral understanding, judgement, and decision. These acts have a personal feel to them; they have a structure that we can all come to know by attending to our own personal experiences. If there is a resource base to which I appeal in these discussions, it is less the list of texts cited in the notes, and more the resource provided by your own efforts to understand your acts of moral knowing.

The selection of Lonergan's thought as the theoretical framework guiding these discussions is not arbitrary. More than any other author, Lonergan makes self-discovery the central activity of philosophy and theology. Lonergan's work focusses on understanding the operations of experiencing, understanding, judging, and deciding as we perform them in our daily routines. While much of his writing is theoretically complex, it is everywhere guided by a single purpose, the understanding of ourselves in our everyday acts of understanding.

Some may object: what do rational processes have to do with the requirements of morality? For the most part, our moral codes and rules have been handed down through cultural and religious traditions. It is often thought that moral codes are divine or that they have more lofty origins than the fallible or self-serving rationality of human minds. What does human knowing have to do with the great moral charters that have commanded the allegiance of civilizations?

The answer to this question is not simple, but the approach here will be direct. While cultural and religious traditions transcend the particularities of time and place, still, they remain fully human. They are the doings of persons. They have their origins in human struggles, human discoveries, and human attempts at understanding – even when they suggest an encounter with the transcendent. Traditions of ethical knowledge have their origins in the efforts of men and women

---

[1] Lonergan's two principal works are *Collected Works of Bernard Lonergan, Vol. 3: Insight*, edited by F. E. Crowe and R. M. Doran (Toronto: University of Toronto Press, 1992; orig. 1957); and *Method in Theology* (New York: Herder & Herder, 1972). For an introduction to other primary texts and secondary literature on Lonergan's work in ethics, see the "Selected Resources on Ethics in the Work of Bernard Lonergan" at the end of this book.

to understand their moral lives. When divine reality is encountered within the orbit of human experience, still, what is passed down through the generations is the testimony of men and women who have sought to understand this encounter and how it affects moral life.[2] This is the work of moral understanding, moral knowing. It may not be the "rationality" we associate with mathematicians or military planners. Nonetheless, it is human knowing.

Some might ask, whose understanding are we considering here? Does this inquiry not beg a prior question? Do people not understand things differently?

To answer this question, you, the reader must become involved. Do you disagree with everyone, all the time, on everything moral or ethical? What about your routines of day-to-day living? Do you not frequently find yourself sharing values, convictions, moral habits, ethical practices with those around you? Even when you disagree, do all of your disagreements end in mortal combat? If not, what do you tacitly agree upon that tempers your disagreeing? These, too, are moral agreements. What about all of those "invisible" value agreements that enable you to participate in routine social activities? Do your lives not involve continual efforts to understand situations and to act responsibly? Do you not seem to manage this routine activity in collaboration with others to some degree of success? How much of your daily responsible living is taken up with the controversial issues and how much remains within the range of the commonly accepted?

What is deceptive about times of great ethical controversy is that they leave us with the illusion that all ethical understanding has broken down. Yet successful moral understanding is going on all the time. In every quarter of our lives, we are sorting out value problems in relationships, working to sustain good institutions, organizing all sorts of individual and group activities in the light of values and goals, and deliberating over "right," "fair," or "just" courses of action for ourselves and others. In each case we do so with a commitment to

---

2    For an introduction to the range of discussions on the relationship between Christian faith and ethics, see C. Curran and R. McCormick, eds., *Readings in Moral Theology, No. 2: The Distinctiveness of Christian Ethics* (New York: Paulist Press, 1980); C. Curran and R. McCormick, eds., *Readings in Moral Theology, No. 7: Natural Law and Theology* (New York: Paulist Press, 1991); Ralph McInerny, *The Question of Christian Ethics* (Washington, D.C.: Catholic University of America Press, 1993).

values and principles that are both intimately personal and publicly shared. All of this involves moral knowing.

While controversial issues tend to lay claim to the meaning of the terms "ethical" and "moral," in reality, these issues are only the tip of an iceberg. We find the bulk of the ethical iceberg in all the normal deliberations and decisions of our everyday living. This massive experience of shared moral living in fact shows how moral knowing "works." Here we seem to be able to do quite a lot of things well. The strategy throughout these pages will be to draw upon an understanding of our successful acts of moral understanding in everyday life to see how we might tackle the problem issues.

One clarification is in order here. Some authors make a distinction between the terms "moral" and "ethical."[3] Ethicists often differ on how to define the terms, however, and frequently the definitions serve to answer specific, technical questions in ethical theory. While these discussions are important for ethicists, the technicalities can often prove confusing for the layperson. For the purposes of this introduction, the terms "ethical" and "moral" will be used inter-changeably to refer, generally, to any experience in our lives when we deliberate and decide how to act. It is true that we often deliberate over technical issues, but technicalities seldom account for the full range of considerations in our deliberations and actions. Usually, our actions aim or intend to achieve objectives, goals, or "goods," and it is this aiming or intending that is our concern through these chapters.

---

3   One view of how the terms "ethical" and "moral" can be differentiated is presented in James J. Walter, "Christian Ethics: Distinctive and Specific?" in *Readings, No. 2: The Distinctiveness of Christian Ethics*, 90–110. Another approach is presented by Paul Ricœur, *Oneself As Another*, trans. K. Blamey (Chicago: University of Chicago Press, 1992) studies 7–8. Other authors argue for a distinction between the terms "right" and "good." See, e.g., John Rawls, *A Theory of Justice* (Cambridge, MA: Harvard University Press, 1971) 446–52. See also William Frankena, "McCormick and the Traditional Distinction," in R. McCormick and P. Ramsey, eds., *Doing Evil to Achieve Good* (Chicago: Loyola University Press, 1978) 146–47. These distinctions are important for advanced theoretical ethics. However, for the purposes of this introductory study, all of these terms will be used interchangeably.

## Moral Knowing as a Skill

Moral knowing is a *skill*, albeit a distinctive one.[4] Ethical understanding and action have a profound impact, not only on our lives, but on those of others. While technical skills seem to involve the manipulation of objects in the external world, ethics seems to go to the heart of persons in quite a different way.

Like other skills, we develop our moral understanding and deciding long before engaging in efforts to reflect, to analyze, to explain what we have been doing. In cultures, moral skills are acquired, developed, implemented in daily living, and passed down from generation to generation, often with little intrusion from the analytic efforts of philosophers or theologians. Like other skills, moral understanding responds to the necessities of everyday living and adapts its existing resources "naturally" to the solution of novel problems.

Using moral skills is quite "natural"; using them consistently and successfully is another matter, however. To do this we must enter the world of theory.[5] The shift to theory is neither uncommon nor unique to ethics. Like other skills, moral understanding is taught most effectively by teachers who have acquired a rather precise technical understanding of skill structure. Good performers or craftspersons often do not make good teachers, because effective teaching requires this additional step beyond skill development, the step to theoretical understanding of the skill itself. Good teachers know that there are ordered patterns to skill development. They spend a great deal of time studying, analysing, and trying to explain these patterns. The result of these efforts is theory.

The need for theory also arises when people encounter new challenges. Theory helps adapt current skills to new tasks. As with playing the piano, using computers, managing an office, cooking, skiing, and running business finances, moral knowing involves complex but

---

4   This presentation draws upon the meaning of the term *skill*, as it is developed by Lonergan in Chapter 2 of *Method*. Lonergan draws upon Jean Piaget for his account of skill development.

5   The term *theory* is often understood negatively, as an impoverished overview of things which we attain when we stand back and view things from a distance. In these chapters, the term is understood differently. Here, theory is an enriched understanding attained when we get insights into relations among ranges of significant details. See Lonergan, *Method*, 81–86.

flexible combinations of basic operations. In each realm, the role of the theorist is to break the skills down into their basic operations and to figure out new adaptations that will allow clusters of operations to yield new strategies in response to new challenges. Once this is done, practice routines can be developed to integrate the new with the old and to get us past blockages.

The goal of these chapters, then, will be to observe how we use the skills of moral understanding in the routines of ordinary life and how we can adapt these skills to the new tasks that lie before us. We will identify the basic operations, how we use them in various combinations, how we distinguish between reliable and unreliable moral insights, and how these successful judgements yield moral knowledge.

### What Difference Does Christian Faith Make?

Up to this point, we have made no mention of Christian faith. The subtitle of this book suggests that this text is directed to those interested in a Christian understanding of ethics. Yet the topic of *faith* arises only in the fourth and fifth chapters. Does this mean that the ethics presented here will simply be another rehash of "humanistic" ethics?

For reasons that will become clearer as we proceed, an explicit discussion of Christian faith will be introduced after a basic presentation of moral knowing. This is not to say that Christian faith is secondary for moral living. Indeed, as the analysis unfolds, it will become apparent that moral knowing and acting are demanding activities, often performed in hostile environments with ambiguous results. They require a formidable commitment. When this commitment is lacking (and even when it is not), adverse conditions, bad judgements, and outright malice often leave their mark on the products. Like all skills, moral living builds upon the achievements of the past and is likewise fettered by past failures. Consequently, the results, for better or worse, accumulate through the ages. These adverse environments, with their demands on commitment and their tendency to accumulate failure, are what the Christian tradition has called *sin*. We will consider the role of Christian faith in ethics in relation to sin.

This line of analysis may seem to run counter to some contemporary trends in Christian theology. Many theologians downplay the significance of sin in ethics. In the main, their efforts have been to dismantle an older view that placed undue emphasis upon sin and guilt and too little upon responsibility and virtue.[6] This is as it should be. Yet to understand Christian faith adequately requires understanding the problems or challenges that gave rise to the faith responses of Christians through the ages. On the whole, Christian faith has emerged as an encounter with Christ amidst people's dramatic experience of suffering and sinfulness. Christian faith is about salvation in Christ, and salvation is deliverance from the reign of sin and evil. Thus a discussion of the debilitating effects of evil introduces the role of Christian faith in moral knowing and acting.

## Moral Knowledge as Social

An approach to Christian ethics that focusses on skills of moral knowing may seem too "individualistic" or "subjectivist." To those who stress the social or cultural context of moral responsibility or the "objective" character of moral knowledge, such an approach may appear misguided. To this charge, I can only respond by saying that the objective, social character of moral knowing should become abundantly clear as we continue.

While we understand the individual human being here as the locus and agent of moral knowing, the objective content of moral knowledge will be shown to be quite real and irreducibly social. In fact, any other approach to moral knowledge makes little sense. Furthermore, no one carries out his or her moral activities in isolation. All of us are embedded in a social environment that shapes our deliberation. Without question, we experience moral values as profoundly personal: they touch the most intimate core of our being. Democratic living requires some measure of individual liberty in ethical decision-making, and moral maturity involves the making of one's "self" through responsible moral action. Nonetheless, the context, the thrust, and the concern of all moral life is objective social life. This is because the primary concern of ethics is living with other people.

The question remains: what do we mean by *social structures*? We often speak of social life in terms of "structures." If we are pressed to

---

6   See Richard Gula, *Reason Informed by Faith* (New York: Paulist Press, 1989); Timothy O'Connell, *Principles for a Catholic Morality*, rev. ed. (San Francisco: Harper & Row, 1990); Stephen Happel and James Walter, *Conversion and Discipleship* (Philadelphia: Fortress Press, 1986).

expand on this image, however, analogies with other kinds of "structure" seem to leave us confused. Social entities are not structures in the sense that buildings or engines or computers are structures. And while organic metaphors often appear more appealing, still, we know that flowers, foxes, and forests involve types of structures that are quite different from societies. What distinguishes social structures from other types of structures is that they are structures of *human meaning*.[7]

Societies are organized routines of meaningful living; they are constituted by shared beliefs, convictions, values, and assumptions; they specify roles according to shared views of common projects, and these roles enter into the sense of identity of persons. All of these involve acts of meaning. Vast ranges of conventions of meaning form the patterns of relations among individual citizens in a society. And wider notions of cosmic order, truth, and justice link the diverse dimensions of human life into the common projects of civilization. None of these events and linkages occur on the level of physics or chemistry. Neither do they occur on the level of botany or zoology. They occur only on the level of human meaning.

To understand social life as meaning, we must determine the way these "structures" operate. What are these "social structures of meaning"? How are the intentions and actions of individuals linked with those of other persons to form recognizable social structures? Do people have to plan these structures of meaning, or can they emerge without anyone planning them? These will be some of the questions that will guide this inquiry into the social character of moral knowledge.

Catholic social ethics, with its emphasis on the "common good,"[8] has influenced the approach to ethics taken here. Ethics is about the good that we build and sustain in common with others. The approach in these chapters, however, adds a twist to more traditionalist notions

---

[7] On the diverse elements, realms, stages, and functions of meaning, see Lonergan, *Method*, Chapter 3.

[8] Two good introductory articles on Catholic social thought and the "common good" can be found in Judith A. Dwyer, ed., *The New Dictionary of Catholic Social Thought* (Collegeville, MN: Liturgical Press, 1994). See David Hollenbach, "Common Good," 192–97; and Michael Schuck, "Modern Catholic Social Thought," 611–32. For a list of relevant introductory articles and texts, see the "Selected Readings on Christian Ethics" at the end of this book.

of the common good, a twist that comes from the work of Lonergan. For many people, the term "the common good" evokes an image of a divinely ordained, static society. The traditionalist image portrays a society in which people have little liberty to define their own identities and their own projects; rather, the overall structure of social life is pre-established, perhaps even enforced by elites, and individuals must "fit in."

The image we adopt is somewhat different. Here, the common good is a dynamic notion, subject to change, and shaped by the participation of all people.[9] Ethical action involves people shaping their own lives and influencing the course of society. The common good is fashioned by all, sets the framework for meeting the requirements of all, and, when it is functioning well, sustains a high degree of liberty for all.[10] Responsibility for the common good requires that individuals evaluate the impact of their actions on the various social structures that constitute this environment. It calls us to choose the public good when the demands of society conflict with our personal desires. In fact, moral maturity means seeking and choosing the common good as a matter of desire and routine habit. To *choose* the common good, however, we must *know* the common good. Moral knowledge, then, is knowledge of the dynamic structure of the common good, how it sustains all aspects of our living, and the demands it makes on our personal decision-making.

**Knowing the Good and Doing the Good**

To this point, we have focussed on moral knowing. Some will object, however, that ethics is not about knowing, but doing. They argue that the requirements of ethics are plain, that the problem is simply that people do not live by what everyone knows to be right. In this view, greed, pride, self-interest, or some other vice is the ethical problem. If

9    On the difference between static and dynamic conceptions of the "common good," see Patrick Byrne, "Jane Jacobs and the Common Good," in F. Lawrence, ed., *Ethics in Making a Living* (Atlanta, GA: Scholars Press, 1989) 169–89.

10   In the past few decades, Christian ethicists have sought to integrate a democratic understanding of the liberty of persons within a theory of the common good. See, e.g., Jacques Maritain, *The Person and the Common Good*, trans. J. J. Fitzgerald (Notre Dame: University of Notre Dame Press, 1966; orig. 1947); and the essays in Oliver Williams and John Houck, eds., *The Common Good and U.S. Capitalism* (Lanham, MD: University Press of America, 1987).

there is a problem of knowledge, it is simply that people who refuse to do the good invariably try to justify their actions with rationalizations.

We need to distinguish two types of moral questions: knowing the good, and doing the good. "What is the good?" concerns moral knowing. "Shall I choose to do the good?" has to do with deciding and acting. To ask the second question presupposes that we have a clear, correct answer to the first; however, our answer to the second can dramatically influence our subsequent ability to answer the first question well.

We are focussing on the first type of question, the question of moral knowledge.[11] Action questions are important, of course, but they presume correct answers to knowledge questions and far too many of these remain poorly answered in our lives. Most of the ethical challenges of our age do, indeed, involve genuine questions for moral knowing. The reason is rooted in the distinction between common-sense moral norms and the theoretical requirements of specific types of moral problems. Common-sense moral norms like "Do not lie!" or "Do not steal!" communicate general moral meaning, but do not specify what counts as lying or stealing in concrete living. We have to understand and deal with real-life moral problems in detail.

When free-trade agreements permit large corporations to gain access to the resources of poorer countries, is this stealing? It depends. Are the negotiations fair? Are the prices sufficient to promote real economic stability, equity, and self-reliance in poorer nations? Will the income benefit the people at large, particularly the poor and the marginalized? Do the contracts include allocations for the adverse environmental effects of resource depletion? These questions, and more, require answers before we arrive at accurate moral knowledge about stealing in such cases. While far too many ethical problems are caused or exacerbated by people who willingly refuse the good, most of the ethical issues of our age involve real problems for moral knowledge. These ethical problems are not simply matters of universal principle or generalized speculation; they are concrete and particular. To act responsibly we must move beyond common-sense norms to

---

[11] As we shall see in the next chapter, there are actually five different types of questions involved in moral deliberation, and attaining reliable moral *knowledge* requires moving back and forth among the first four of these types of questions.

accurate ethical knowledge. Hence the need to know how we answer questions for moral knowing.

One final point: this distinction between two types of moral questions is exceedingly important. Most of us have learned to think about ethics in terms of the second type of question. When moral problems arise, our first inclination is often to find out who is to blame for doing wrong. This inclination, however, presupposes that we already know what is right and what is wrong in this situation. Quite often, this is not the case, but our habits lead us to jump over the first question and focus on the second. To engage authentically in ethical inquiry requires the honest admission that sometimes we do not already know the answers. For those of us who think of ethics as questions for action and blame, this admission takes a good deal of self-discipline.[12]

## Itinerary

The chapters unfold in two parts. Part One, Chapters 1, 2 and 3, invites us on a journey of self-discovery. It is the discovery of ourselves in our operations of moral knowing. Chapter 1 focusses on the general experience of moral responsibility and the operations which unfold in our deliberations and actions. While these operations have a general structure, they also function within horizons of meaning that both illuminate and conceal elements of our moral experience.

Chapter 2 examines the social character of the object of these operations, moral knowledge. Moral knowledge has a range of rather odd features, best understood through a set of contrasting images. Next, we explore three distinct levels of meaning of moral language. Finally, we explore a novel way of understanding "social structures" and examine how actions informed by the three levels of moral meaning shape our participation in these structures.

In Chapter 3, the focus is on ourselves as subjects of these operations. In particular, we examine how we are constituted and subtly transformed as social persons through these operations. Insights into this process yield a novel way of understanding human freedom. Understanding and appropriating this process of meaning-making

---

12 For further discussion on the role of diverse types of questions in moral deliberation, see Kenneth R. Melchin, "Moral Decision-Making and the Role of the Moral Question," *METHOD: Journal of Lonergan Studies* 11 (1993): 215–28.

can provide fundamental norms or obligations to guide us in wrestling with moral issues.

Part Two, Chapters 4 and 5, investigates how Christian faith shapes our involvement in the operations of moral knowing. Chapter 4 introduces faith, not as a set of general principles, beliefs or convictions, but as a response to a universal problem: sin. Sin is not simply acts of ill-will; more significantly, it involves structures that limit and distort our habits of moral meaning and, thus, our capacities for moral knowledge and action. Faith is the encounter with God's saving grace which reverses the debilitating cycles of moral deformation that unfold through sin.

Chapter 5 explores a range of insights into the way that faith forms our operations of moral deliberation: insights into God's justice, the dignity of the person, the common good, and the preferential option for the poor. Faith is not a set of principles containing logical implications for concrete situations. We must still implement the operations and skills of moral understanding and judgement in concrete contexts. Rather, Christian faith exercises a *heuristic* force that moves moral inquiry in a specific direction, and with a characteristic set of concerns.

The guiding concern through all of these chapters is the quest for self-knowledge. Our richest resource for insights in ethics is our own moral experiences. Typically, we are preoccupied with the general, day-to-day flow of images and insights in our experience. Most of us, however, seldom attend to the *operations* of meaning that beget these experiences. Furthermore, we seldom plumb the hidden depths of ourselves as subjects of these operations of meaning. For most of us, this inner realm remains a mystery.

These chapters are only a beginning. It still remains to harness these insights and bring them to bear upon the complex moral problems of our age. I hope that, in attending to our everyday activities of moral deliberation and action, we will discover the foundations for moving collectively beyond the impasses in contemporary public ethical debates.

# PART ONE

# MORAL KNOWING
# AND MORAL PERSONS

## Chapter 1

# The Experience of Moral Responsibility

Take a moment to imagine[13] that you are on vacation, stretched out on a vast expanse of magnificent white beach, with no one around for miles. You are finally getting that relief from the tension and anxiety of daily life that you most certainly deserve. You can feel your muscles relaxing. You can feel the stress flowing out of your body. You can feel your mind detaching from everyday concerns, releasing the grip of concentrated attention. Your mind begins to wander, to float blissfully, to be carried here, then there, from one pleasant image to another, on the breezes that blow in that familiar region of consciousness between waking and sleeping.

Suddenly a scream breaks through your state of bliss.

"Help!!!"

Your entire being suddenly shifts into gear! You are transformed! In a single movement your body and mind rise together into a state of action, of focussed attention, of total concentration. It is as different from your previous state as a hurricane from a calm summer's day. Before, you were at rest. Now you are in motion! You are energized! You are dynamized by a concern, a desire, a commitment to action. Who screamed? Are they drowning? Where are they? How to help them? Find out! Get to them! Save them! Keep them alive!

What has happened to you?

The most important step in understanding moral knowledge and moral action is discovering that behind the familiar objects of our experience lies an inner realm which is quite strange. This is the realm of ourselves as subjects. Most of our lives we spend experiencing

---

13   This exercise is a reconstruction of a self-appropriation activity first introduced to me in a course by Philip McShane at Concordia University, Lonergan College, in 1978–79. Similar exercises are presented by McShane in *Process* (Lanham, Md: University Press of America, 1997) and *Wealth of Self and Wealth of Nations* (Hicksville, N.Y.: Exposition Press, 1975).

things, examining things, doing things, with our attention focussed on the things before us. Yet all the while we are being moved through our actions by invisible inner forces and operations that subtly evade our attention; these are the forces and operations of the experiencing, the examining, the doing themselves.

The forces do not come from outside us, but rather from inside. And while we often play a deliberate role in mobilizing or guiding the operations, still they have an energy and a direction of their own that almost invisibly carry us through much of our lives. To understand moral responsibility requires that we turn our attention away from the objects of our experience and towards these ever-present forces and operations that carry us through the various stages of responsible action. For most of us, this is unfamiliar terrain. It is the terrain of self as mystery.

Our imagined event on the beach can provide us with an opportunity to attend to this inner realm wherein lie the foundations of moral action. For most of us, events like this are familiar. We can all recall times when we have responded to the call of another in need, when we have been moved into action by a sense of responsibility. What can we observe about such events?

## Getting a Feel for Responsibility

First, on the beach we experienced a transformation. It was a transformation from one state of being to another. It was a transformation, not simply in the objects of our attention, but in our entire state of attention, in our way of engaging in experience. In both states we were conscious and we were experiencing, but there was a difference. This difference was not in *what* we experienced, but in *how*. The new state had a different pattern, a different order, a different feeling, a different energy level, a different way of focussing on its objects, a different architecture.

Second, there is something odd about what "caused" this transformation. Surely the call for help coming from outside played a significant role, but this cannot be all. How could such a "cause" have such an enormous "effect" on us? Why did this sound evoke this reaction while another sound, say for example, a "mew!", evokes something totally different? We do not find the key elements of the answer in the physical structure of the sounds; we find them inside us. The call "mobilized" or evoked a dynamism from within us to respond to another in need. The forces that dynamized this response form part of that all-too-familiar set of interior forces or operations that make us what we are and propel us through moral experience.[14]

Third, one of the key elements that differentiates the first state from the second is motion or action. If we can characterize our first state as rest, disengagement, peace, and tranquillity, we can describe the second as a state of motion, focussed concern, heightened intensity, and action.

Fourth, this motion was directed somewhere, towards an aim or an objective. Yet the objective functioned in a very odd way to direct the motion. Even when we were not sure of the source of the sound, we were catapulted into action, first to understand and verify what it was, where it was, and what to do, and then to act on this knowledge. We may not have been sure if the sound really was a person drowning. Still, we were mobilized towards finding out. Once we were sure, our questions shifted to focus on the actions involved in saving them. The precise object of the forces that propel us into moral action are often not known or clearly present to us in advance. Indeed, the opposite is true. The interior forces or operations of moral responsibility set us in motion not simply to attain an objective, but also to determine the precise form of the objective itself.

Fifth, while the motion that characterized this state of action was clearly conscious and involved deliberate action, we did not initiate the motion itself by deliberate action. On the contrary, when we heard the call we were moved spontaneously into a variety of operations, few, if any of which, we would have explicitly chosen. Deliberation and choice came into play along the way, but they too were mobilized by a more basic dynamism. While we might have self-consciously chosen our strategy for saving the person, we did not deliberately choose to be curious about the sound, to care for the drowning person, to set in motion the questioning and answering which, finally, resulted in our strategy.

Sixth, this motion that carried us through the whole process was charged with feeling. The dynamic that propelled us forward was a sense of care or responsibility for the drowning person, and this responsibility could take hold of us so dramatically because it was

---

[14] Lonergan uses the term "intentionality" to refer to this dynamism which mobilizes us in relation to objects of experience. See *Method*, 6–13.

saturated with feeling. Again, we did not deliberately choose these feelings; rather, they seemed to choose us and animate us. In addition, the feelings seemed to have a distinctive flavour or texture that came from our response to the drowning person. A "roar!" a "help!" and a "mew!" feel different because of our different relationships with the sources of the sounds. It is as if the feelings help to guide us, to hone us in on the goal, and it is the texture and flavour of the feelings that seem to play a distinctive role in this guiding.

Finally, while this dynamism of responsibility arises in us spontaneously, before conscious choice, and is quite universal, shared by most people throughout much of life, it is by no means fully automatic or guaranteed. There is an element of learning or acquired habit that plays a crucial role in determining if and when responsibility will arise in us, how strongly it will affect us, and what form it will take. If we really work at it or if we are traumatized, our feelings of responsibility towards others can be dulled. By contrast, we can play a role in developing habits of caring and discernment in ourselves and our children so that, in instances like this, the motions dynamizing responsible action arise consistently and vigorously.

What, then, is the significance of all of this for ethics?

The goal of this exercise has been to launch our study of moral knowledge and action by directing our attention to a dynamism of care or moral "outwardness" that we can be observe in our personal lives.[15] Moral experiences are charged with feelings of care which have the effect of directing our attention outwards. In addition, while we often formulate moral rules in terms of obligations imposed by others, this focus on the authority of others can be quite misleading. To understand moral life fully requires attending to the basic experience of responsibility itself as a dynamism of care that is revealed to us in our own moral action. Here is where we discover the foundations of ethics.[16]

---

[15] Lonergan uses the terms "transcendental" and "self-transcending" to refer to the way in which operations of knowing and valuing "go beyond" extant states of knowledge and value to attain new knowledge and new states of virtue. See *Method*, 11–13, 30–36.

[16] Lonergan's presentation of the elements for a theory of ethics can be found in *Insight*, Chapters 6, 7, and 18; and *Method*, Chapter 2. For an introduction to

This exercise is also important because it can help us correct something in the way we commonly think about moral responsibility. Most of us were taught morals as rules, regulations, and obligations formulated by others, usually authority figures, which are imposed upon us to force us to act (usually begrudgingly) in socially acceptable ways. There are elements of truth in this image, but what this image fails to portray is a prior, more basic interior grounding to morality that accounts both for the origin of the rules themselves and for the way in which they function in our own lives. This grounding is a more basic care or outwardness which social teaching harnesses and directs.

For the most part, moral rules arise in societies as a consequence of people's efforts to respond to problems, to care for others, to prevent social tragedies, to protect weaker members from exploitation, and, generally, to coordinate people into common action to accomplish and sustain what none could achieve on their own. While the rules may be passed down to us as obligations arising from outside, these rules came into being because people were dynamized originally by an interior drive of responsibility similar to what we observed in ourselves in our "beach" experiment.

Furthermore, parents, teachers, and mentors in social life seek to promote and instill moral rules out of a sense of personal responsibility which is another manifestation of this inner exigency or dynamism that moved us into action on the beach. Finally, when others teach us moral rules, the reason they can take such a hold on us is that the teaching elicits this dynamic of responsibility in us and works with it. Teaching focusses responsibility and nurtures it; it does not create or impose it.[17] Moral "socialization" harnesses this dynamic that is operative in us and directs it towards objectives devised and chosen by others who were mobilized by a similar interior motion.

---

discussions of the relation between *Insight* (1957) and *Method* (1972), see Frederick E. Crowe, "An Exploration of Lonergan's New Notion of Value," in M. Vertin, ed., *Appropriating the Lonergan Idea* (Washington, D.C.: Catholic University of America Press, 1989) 51–70; and Kenneth R. Melchin, "Ethics in *Insight*," in F. Lawrence, ed., *Lonergan Workshop*, vol. 8 (Atlanta, GA: Scholars Press, 1990) 135–47.

[17] For a fascinating discussion of the role of this dynamism of the intentional operations in education, see Lonergan, *Topics in Education*, vol. 10 of *The Collected Works of Bernard Lonergan*, edited by R. M. Doran and F. E. Crowe (Toronto: University of Toronto Press, 1993).

## Facts and Values: The Operations of Moral Questioning

In situations like this, where we respond immediately and vigorously to help another person in need, our actions often seem to unfold as a single motion. From rest we move immediately into action to locate the source of the cry, to move towards it, to deliver the person from danger, and to ensure his or her safekeeping. The apparent unity of this action is deceptive, however; it conceals an inner complexity. The total project involves our coordinating a rather large set of operations in service of a single objective. And if any one of these operations is missing, the project grinds to a halt. We can be dedicated, we can be a good swimmer, we can have good resuscitation skills, and we can have the strength to haul in a drowning person, but if we cannot locate the person, we are powerless to attain our objective.

Moral actions might look like single, unified operations, but actually they are rather complex chains of operations.[18] When every link is present, the appearance of unity is preserved, but when one link is missing, we see the true inner complexity. In this respect, moral action resembles a skill like learning to drive a car. If we have mastered the skill, our actions seem smooth, unified, effortless. If we have not, our actions become a choppy, halting movement, first through one step, then on to another, only to discover that we have missed a step and the car has stalled.

Some of the operations involved in moral action are skills like those we might learn as a lifeguard or as a medical practitioner. Yet the basic operations of moral responsibility are of a different sort. They involve operations of questioning. In fact, we often do not formulate our questions. Commonly, they involve little more than a glance to wonder at this, a turn of the head to confirm that, an argument with another person to settle on a strategy, or an examination of the situation to determine if the strategy is viable. Nonetheless, acts of questioning drive all of these gestures. And an examination of different kinds of questions can help us better understand the links in the chain of moral responsibility.

---

[18] Lonergan uses the term "recurrence scheme" to explain the linking of events into circular schemes or systems. See *Insight*, Chapter 4.2; Philip McShane, *Randomness, Statistics and Emergence* (Dublin: Gill and Macmillan, 1970); Kenneth R. Melchin, *History, Ethics, and Emergent Probability* (Lanham, MD: University Press of America, 1987); and "History, Ethics, and Emergent Probability," in F. Lawrence, ed., *Lonergan Workshop*, vol. 7 (Atlanta, GA: Scholars Press, 1988) 269–94.

The most basic question which transformed us from our state of rest and set us in motion on the beach was the *what* question:[19] "What is making that sound?" "What is it?" In this instance, we might easily have settled on the answer to this question. In many instances, answering this question to our satisfaction is not so simple. Often, the "what?" question is met, not by one single answer, but by a host of different answers: "It is a seagull!" "It is a radio!" "It is an animal!" "It is someone stealing my car!" "It is someone drowning!" When this is the case, the *what* question begins to reveal its limitations. It may be that finding a satisfactory answer to the *what* question requires continually multiplying answers until we stumble on one that "fits." More often, finding the satisfactory answer requires dropping this question and asking a different kind of question, the question for selection and judgement.

This second kind of question we will call the *is it so* question: "Is it this, or is it that?" Notice that this question does not ask for anything new in the line of possible candidates for answers. Rather, this question seeks to scrutinize each entry on the list of candidates, to consult the data on the situation, to recall the original intent of the *what* question, and to find a "fit." Here, of course, the word "fit" has a complex meaning which can differ, depending on the type of inquiry. In general, by "fit" we mean that: (i) the question and the proposed answer together specify a set of conditions that must be fulfilled for the answer to "fit" the question (if it's a person drowning, we should be able to see something like splashing in the direction from which we heard the sound); (ii) we determine whether, in fact, these conditions are fulfilled by the evidence (it is a person drowning because I can see splashing in the water in the same direction from which the sound is coming); and (iii) we rule out the other proposed answers because the

---

19 The account of the operations involved in knowledge of fact and knowledge of value which is presented here is somewhat different from that which is typically portrayed by Lonergan scholars. This account is based on the work of Philip McShane. See *Wealth of Self*, 11–16, 47–53; and *Process*, Chapter 2.5. For an introduction to other discussions of the operations and levels relevant to ethics, see Patrick Byrne, "Consciousness: Levels, Sublations, and the Subject as Subject," *METHOD: Journal of Lonergan Studies* 13 (1995): 131–50; Michael Vertin, "Judgments of Value, for the Later Lonergan," *METHOD: Journal of Lonergan Studies* 13 (1995): 221–48. For a discussion of differences among Lonergan scholars on this issue, see Joseph Cassidy, "Extending Bernard Lonergan's Ethics" (Ph.D. dissertation, Saint Paul University, Ottawa, 1995).

evidence does not fulfill their conditions (it's not a radio because there's no possible location for a radio visible for miles on the beach; it's not a seagull because the sky is clear and there are no seagulls visible anywhere).[20]

When the conditions and the supporting evidence are immediately known, the *what* and *is it so* questions appear as one single operation. The duality becomes clear when we cannot fulfill one of the two conditions easily, as in the example of learning to drive a car. We stumble. This is when we have to set about judging which candidates qualify as answers, or, perhaps if none qualify, we have to return to the *what* question for more candidates.

So far, on the face of it, there does not seem to be anything distinctively "moral" or "ethical" about these questions or their answers. These seem to be ordinary questions settling matters of "fact." This is quite so. It is important to notice, however, that in this case where a person is drowning (quite obviously a moral concern), "fact" questions take on a special feeling of urgency to them. While we can feel this urgency from the very outset, the distinctive feature of this feeling becomes clear once we have settled on answers. In a situation where the exigence of moral responsibility carries us forward, answers to "fact" questions do not leave us satisfied. In fact, once we have the "fact" answers, we seem to be propelled into quite a different set of questions: "What to do?"

This realm of "act" questions is the properly moral or ethical realm. Like the "fact" questions, there are two types of "act" questions, the *what* questions and the *is it so* questions. Only this time, the questioning intends goals or objectives that are quite different. Now, the "what?" means "What do I do?" and the "Is it so?" means "Is this the right thing to do?" There is a similarity in structure to the "fact" questions in that the *what* questions usually result in a variety of possible candidates for answers, and the *is it so* question seeks to select the one that "fits." The big difference lies in the way in which the answers "fit" the questions and the data on the situation.

While the "fact" questions seek to know something that has already occurred, the "act" questions seek to bring into being something that

---

[20]  Lonergan's account of judgements of fact is considerably more detailed than the introductory account presented here. See *Insight*, Chapters 9, 10, and 11.

has not yet occurred, our own action.[21] This makes the task of getting a "fit" among the answer, the question, and the data somewhat more complex. The subsequent chapters of this book will be devoted to helping us understand how we do this. For the present purposes, however, some of these observations should help us get a general idea of the various types of questions involved in moral action.

The basic thrust of "act" questions is to come up with strategies for action that have not yet occurred. While others have saved drowning persons in the past, the act question is utterly concrete and personal; it asks if I am to do such a thing in this situation, right now, in the most immediate future. Still, "act" questioning does have a concern with the past and the present. Ethics frequently scrutinizes past actions to sort out success from failure or right from wrong. It is important to notice, however, what we are doing in such scrutiny. The concern that drives the moral evaluation of past action is not a concern for settling matters of fact. Instead, we want to return in thought to the time before that past action and grasp why someone chose that course of action then, so that this reasoning can guide us in our future acting. To say that something was "right" is to say that the person "should have done that," that this future action should have been brought into being at that time, and that in similar cases in the future we should act accordingly. It is this concern with the future, with action, that gives moral questioning its distinctive character.

When we raise and answer "act" questions, we are understanding and judging moral values.[22] Values that are passed down through the generations and taught to children are tried and true answers to "act" questions that help us to act in future situations in ways that "fit" the general requirements of communal living. Such values provide us with strategies for living with other people. While we have presented "act" questions as following on "fact" questions, generally we move back and forth in our inquiry. When we know the facts, we are moved to act in one way or another. As we discover what others have valued in the past, and what we too value, we often return to our assessment

21  On the future orientation of moral questions, see *Insight*, Chapters 18.2.3 and 18.2.4; see also Melchin, "Ethics in *Insight*."

22  For a discussion of the various elements involved in judgements of value, see Vertin, "Judgments of Value"; Melchin, "Ethics in *Insight*"; and *History, Ethics, and Emergent Probability*, 195–99.

of the "facts" to find dimensions of reality that were previously hidden from view. Value or "action" concerns thus drive this search for facts. When our concerns are transformed, we are often sent back to ask about "facts" in search of new data, with new questions, guided by new hunches.

"Act" questions (both of the *what* type and the *is it so* type) reveal a further step in the chain of operations of moral action. Just as answers to "fact" questions leave us unsettled in situations of moral responsibility, so too do "act" questions. This is because the goal of "act" questions is not simply moral knowledge; it is moral action. The last stage in the sequence or scheme involves a new type of questioning altogether, one that does not seek knowledge, but which is nonetheless a questioning in its own right. This last stage is the exigency or drive to "do it!"[23]

We might think that the word "questioning" is inappropriate for the *do it* stage. On further examination, however, we see that this stage is similar to the other operations of questioning. First, we experience it as a drive that moves us into operation. Second, we obtain results only as we follow through on the exigency or questioning. Third, there is an element of indeterminacy or uncertainty, for there is no guarantee we will launch the activity or follow through and attain the objective of the operation. Finally, moral decision requires that we settle a "yes or no" type of question. Will I do it or not? When we have decided, the question is answered; action follows.

What is clearly different about our questions at the *do it* stage is that we do not end up with knowledge alone (either factual knowledge or moral knowledge). If I am concerned only with what I know ("Am I going to act on this or not?" "Perhaps yes, probably not!"), I can have that knowledge without acting on it. Yet this would not really be knowledge of the future; instead, it is knowledge about what I am like, my habits or virtue, whether I am the sort of person who acts in this way. This knowledge does not involve that exigency or drive to "do it" that is central to decision-making. When we decide, we transform moral knowledge into reality by taking the answers to the "act" questions ("This is what I definitely should do!") and doing them. When we do this, we are responding to an inner demand that

---

[23] This is what Lonergan calls the "decision." See *Insight*, Chapter 18.2.5; *Method*, Chapter 1.2.

our doing be consistent with our knowing: do we have integrity?; are we willing to live up to our convictions?

In summary, we can say that moral action is not a single movement from experience to action; instead, it is a complex chain or scheme of operations, each of which is driven by a distinctive type of questioning. It is the question operative at each stage in the process that gives that stage its distinctive features and specifies the requirements that the operations must fulfill. Unlike the forces that drive an engine or a computer, this questioning does not ensure either that we carry out the operation or that we achieve success. The exigency of questioning is a distinctive *urge, force,* or *power.* Though it is a *drive* towards a goal, that goal is not precisely defined or determined. To understand ethics requires getting a feel for the unique features of this exigency or drive, for it is different from most forces that we meet in life.

Two types of questions arise in us: "fact" questions and "act" or value questions. To act, we must know the facts. New strategies for action, however, can set us in search of new facts. With both "act" and "fact" questioning we find a further division. *What* questions evoke answers, but possible answers can multiply indefinitely. If we want to *know,* we have to ask, "Is it so?" or "Is it right?" This inquiry scrutinizes the range of possible answers in search of links between the question, the answer, and the evidence. Finally, moral knowledge calls for moral action, but that does not necessarily mean we will act. So there remains the question whether we will act consistently with our deliberations. Here we can resolve the issue of integrity, the final step in the scheme of moral responsibility, only if we give ourselves over to this exigency, and act.

## Horizons, Cultures, and Conversions

In recent centuries we have discovered a significant feature of knowledge and responsibility which has changed the way we understand moral life. This is the feature we call "moral horizons." The term "horizon" refers generally to the limits of what we can see from a given vantage point.[24] Horizons, however, are not only visual,

---

[24] Lonergan's discussions of "horizons" are sprinkled throughout his various works. For an introductory discussion, see *Method,* 77, 220–24, 235–37; and *Topics in Education,* 88–91.

they are also moral or ethical: from our particular vantage points or points of view we encounter limits in what we can habitually value or care about.

Interestingly, the limits that define the boundaries of our field of vision or valuing are not themselves "visible." Like the dynamism of moral responsibility itself, horizons are just beyond our field of explicit awareness. Still, they exert a dramatic impact upon our day-to-day living. And as we find with learning the skills of driving a car or saving a drowning person, we start to notice these horizons when things go wrong.

Often we discover our moral horizons when we meet someone from a different culture. If you have had to live closely with someone from another culture, doubtless you have noticed that they seem to have different priorities. Some things they seem to value too highly. Others, which we think important, they seem not to care about at all. It is as if they were living their lives around a different centre. Perhaps they pay too little attention to mowing the lawn or spend far too much time with uncles, aunts, and cousins (who always park cars in your spot). Perhaps they show too little concern when their cat digs up your flowers, or they spend too much time cooking (with all of those awful smells).

On reflection, what we are seeing in such situations (if we are honest with ourselves) is not simply *their* moral and cultural horizons, but *our own* as well. We find that the two do not "fit," because the previously invisible aspects of our horizons are clashing with the all-too-visible features of theirs. To be sure, this clash is unsettling. If we can move beyond the initial irritation and ask ourselves what, in our lives, is clashing with theirs and why we value these ways of living, we can begin to map out the terrain and the boundaries of our own moral horizons. If we launch this project in earnest, it can have some startling results, including, perhaps, a subtle shifting of these boundaries and restructuring of the terrain in our lives. Self-knowledge can lead to real growth in moral maturity.

Horizons mark the difference between what we care for and value, and what we deem secondary, irrelevant, or inappropriate. We make these divisions in two ways. We can allow the secondary concerns into our field of conscious attention, but brush them aside. More frequently, however, horizons screen out the secondary entirely. We filter out of the field of conscious attention the "secondary," "irrelevant," or "inappropriate," and relegate it to an inaccessible limbo. In this second case, what we screen out are not simply data or answers to questions, but, more significantly, the very ability or habit of caring for cherished ways of living. Such screening happens, for example, when soldiers who are traumatized in war find themselves without the tools for living in peacetime, unable to care for the things that others value. When horizons function in this second way, they become doubly invisible: not only are they unnoticed, hanging like a backdrop in our mental landscape, but they also block out the terrain that would reveal their locations.

While people of different cultures can see the diversity of their respective moral horizons fairly easily, friends and loved ones from similar backgrounds have more difficulty detecting them. It is often in situations of conflict or argument that we can observe differences in moral horizons. In most arguments the parties focus entirely on their own explicit positions. Behind these positions, however, lie the horizons of concern and value that ground them.[25] Because moral horizons operate before we begin thinking, as the background for our explicit positions, they are usually the last things that we discuss in an argument. Consequently, our moral horizons often spontaneously screen out the concerns that animate the other person. To attain some resolution requires valuing the very thing that our own horizon is screening out. This is true for the other person as well. If we ever do succeed in breaking this deadlock, it is often because events, gestures, or actions (rather than words) break through our horizon to show us that a deeply held concern of theirs is worth valuing.

When we analyze the phenomenon of moral horizons, we find three realms of value.[26]

(i) *The Known.* Here, of course, the "known" does not simply imply answers to "fact" questions, but also answers to "act" or value questions. We have come to know, understand, and care about particular values as well as *dis*values, things we know to be bad.

---

[25] For a fascinating presentation of this distinction between positions and underlying concerns and their relevance to conflicts, see Cheryl A. Picard, *Campus Mediation Training Manual* (Ottawa: Carleton University Press, 1993).

[26] This account is drawn from Lonergan, *Topics in Education,* 88–91. See also Walter Conn, *Conscience: Development and Self-Transcendence* (Birmingham: Religious Education Press, 1981) 127–30.

(ii) *The Known Unknown.* This seems like a contradiction, but in fact all of us deal regularly with matters that we have not come to understand and appropriate personally, but which we know to be part of the fund of common knowledge. So, in the realm of ethics we may not understand issues of justice in international conflicts, but we do know that international agencies have formulated standards of conduct for member countries and we can care for their goals and objectives.

(iii) *The Unknown Unknown.* This is the region that lies completely beyond our horizons of knowing and caring; here we cannot even ask the questions. Our ignorance here can wreak the most havoc in moral analysis and action, particularly if we remain unaware or refuse to acknowledge this ignorance in principle. The most significant moral horizon is the boundary between the Known Unknown and the Unknown Unknown.

The process in which horizons move back to embrace elements that previously were beyond our imagining, we will call *conversion.*[27] Religious traditions have spoken a great deal about religious conversion, but the conversion we are referring to here need not involve explicitly religious elements; rather, it is any course of events in which horizons in one's life are pushed back.

Conversion does not mean simply that we start imagining new things as objects of our care and concern, but that these objects *reorder our moral landscape.* As we discover new values, we give higher priority to old actions and events, old memories take on new meaning, and other events and actions previously thought important retreat into the shadows of insignificance. Familiar things become strangely new. New-found things, eagerly anticipated in the past, become boring and irrelevant. We begin to feel clumsy doing familiar things because we have discovered a dimension to them that we had previously overlooked and undervalued. Impossible things become possible.

---

[27] Lonergan presents the topic of "conversion" in *Method*, Chapter 10.2, and in numerous other essays. For an introductory discussion of the notion of "conversion" in Lonergan and in other authors, see Walter Conn, *Conscience;* and Walter Conn, ed., *Conversion* (New York: Alba House, 1978). See also numerous other essays on the topic published by Lonergan scholars in the various edited collections and journals listed in the "Selected Resources on Ethics in the Work of Bernard Lonergan," at the end of this book.

This picture of things is a bit too rosy; in real life, most conversions or transformations are not the restructuring of our entire lives. Instead, they are partial, and often occur gradually. Further, conversion entails struggle: while the effects of conversion can be awesome and liberating, the steps of conversion themselves are usually quite painful. Moral horizons exclude elements from our conscious awareness for a reason: without a basic psychic order to our living we would go crazy. Being open to conversion means risking a breakdown in this order. If we want to grow as adult persons, we must recognize that this painful restructuring will always be part of life.

## Feelings and Moral Value

We must address one final topic before we examine the characteristics of moral knowledge in detail. This is the topic of feelings. Often in our society, ethics is portrayed as a personal conviction that expresses our feelings towards things. Philosophers have spoken of ethics as "moral sentiments" and, in some cases, have argued that ethical principles express nothing more than our feelings towards things. If things are of value, it is because we have attributed feelings of value to them. Our moral feelings are diverse, and, so it is argued, we have a democratic right to our own feelings. Some would even claim that there is no objective content to ethics beyond the feelings that are evoked in us and expressed in our moral language.[28] This philosophy or assumption is quite prevalent in our culture and often leads us to misunderstand moral responsibility.

Like most philosophical positions or arguments, this view emerged historically in the context of a debate with another position and was formulated to correct problems or excesses in that other position. This other claim was that moral values derive their meaning and truth from a universal objective order, established once and for all in the universe, which humanity plays little role in authoring, and into which we must fit by discerning the logic of the "grand design." In this view of things, feelings belonged on the lowest level of human life (in no small measure because this was thought to be the realm of

---

[28] For an extended critical discussion of "emotivism" and its historical legacy, see Alasdair MacIntyre, *After Virtue*, 2nd ed. (Notre Dame: University of Notre Dame Press, 1984).

the "feminine"); this was the level shared by the beasts, the level which must always be mastered by intellect.

To correct this view, the challengers made two observations: (i) humanity plays a significant role in establishing the designs of history and culture, and we are responsible for doing this properly; and (ii) what we thought was the mastery of feelings was, in large measure, the perversion of feelings.[29] If we are going to take responsibility for history, they said, we need to acknowledge and cultivate the realm of feelings and to get them back on track.

As with all revolutions, however, this one began to devour its own children. What was first articulated as a corrective to a flaw in another position became enshrined as an absolute principle. Feelings were no longer merely a part of ethics: they were now thought to be the whole of ethics. While the notions of objectivity articulated by the earlier opponents certainly had to be corrected, the new, "emotivist" approaches would take the bold step of repudiating entirely the moral "objectivity" of the values that are the object of our feelings. Thus we live today in the debris left by this historical struggle.

What, then, are we to make of feelings, their role in moral knowledge and their significance for moral objectivity? As a point of departure, we can make a number of observations which can be verified in our own lives.

First, in the examples given above we found that feelings arise and animate the various operations in moral questioning. Indeed, we experience the exigence or drive of moral responsibility itself as a strong feeling, and each of the operations in moral inquiry and action are charged with a distinctive feeling of their own.

There are various types of feelings, however, and not all types play the same role in moral knowing and doing.[30] In the operations described above, the feelings could be called self-transcending. They point beyond themselves and focus our concern on their objects, carrying us out of ourselves, beyond our feelings, into further

---

[29] Lonergan analyses this process of responsibly shaping history as an activity of meaning, and he differentiates the "efficient" and "constitutive" functions of meaning in history. See *Method*, 77–78. On the need for coming to terms with one's feelings for moral authenticity, see Lonergan, *Method*, 30–34.

[30] Mark Doorley presents an extended discussion of the diverse types of feeling and their roles in Lonergan's ethics in *The Place of the Heart in Lonergan's Ethics* (Lanham, MD: University Press of America, 1996).

operations that seek moral knowledge and action. When we answer "fact" and "act" questions, we do so with feeling, but the feelings are not the criteria for the moral validity of the knowledge and action.

Second, there is another class of morally relevant feelings that do play a more substantial role in moral knowing and acting but, again, which do not exhaust either the criteria or the meaning of moral claims. These feelings can be called "intentional responses to values."[31] Quite frequently we act on something like a hunch, a desire, or a fear. We cannot explain these feelings, nor can we validate them. Often we cannot even express them in the proper words. Nonetheless, they carry us into action in a specific direction, towards a value which, at the beginning, we could not articulate. If we move with the feeling through the process of moral understanding, often we begin to discover the value towards which the feeling was directing us. The texture of the feeling acted as something like a guidance mechanism to direct us towards the value. Once we know the value and make it our own, the feeling remains, to keep our thought and action moving in line with it.

In cases like this, the feeling does not make the value; rather, it merely indicates a value which is valid in its own right. One of the problems with feelings is that they can be mistaken, and the only way we can find this out is by asking and answering questions for moral knowledge. If we want to cultivate virtues, we must cultivate morally excellent feelings. In the final analysis, however, the object of the feeling can be known and verified as such only through the operations of moral knowing.

## Summary

Where have these reflections taken us? Let us take stock of the observations we have made on this initial journey into self-understanding.

Our first observation concerned the exigence of moral responsibility: our sense of moral responsibility does not come from outside of us. It arises as a feeling-charged exigence or dynamism erupting from within, which propels us outward with a care for the objects of experience, with an interest or concern for action in response to persons, things and events in the world. This inner dynamic does not pronounce the last word on moral right or wrong, but it does set in motion the

---

[31] See Lonergan, *Method*, 30–34.

subsequent operations of reflection and evaluation which will carry out this task. It is not an ineluctable "cause" which systematically yields "effects"; rather, it is an exigence or inclination which can be heeded or ignored, cultivated or squelched. Nonetheless, it is an exigence, an inner urgency, and it sets in motion the very operations of reflection and decision-making that would heed, ignore, cultivate, or squelch.

Our second observation concerned the operations of moral meaning that are set in motion by the exigence of responsibility. In any instance, moral knowing is not a single act, but a cluster or chain of five distinct acts which work together to move us towards knowledge and the actuation of value: the acts of understanding and judging facts, the acts of understanding and judging value, and the act of decision. The characteristic form of each of these operations is that of questioning, and each act of questioning has its distinctive object. Like the exigence of responsibility itself, each question is presented to us as an urgent demand to be accepted or refused, rather than as a mechanical "cause" yielding inevitable "effects." In following these exigences and in cultivating the skills of responding in diverse areas of experience, we develop the full range of capacities for responsible moral action.

We made a third observation on the subject of horizons. The operations of moral meaning do not yield single, isolated meanings; they yield clusters of meanings which form coherent wholes. They also set patterns of anticipation that direct further acts of questioning. These coherent wholes or fields of moral meaning have boundaries or horizons. Horizons limit what we ask questions about and, consequently, what we can know. More significantly for moral life, they delimit the range of what we habitually care about. We can see the limitations of horizons when they break down, and we find ourselves experiencing and caring about things which previously were screened out. This "conversion" process may happen infrequently, but it can also be encouraged and cultivated so that we come to live in anticipation of ever-new encounters with the "unknown unknown."

Our final observation was about feelings. We found that feelings have a significant first role and a series of intermediate roles in moral knowing, and that all of the operations of moral questioning, including the basic exigence of responsibility itself, are charged with feeling.

We also observed, however, that some feelings point beyond themselves: they lead us to ask questions so that we may discover and assess their objects. Feelings of this type – intentional responses to values – set us in motion through the various operations of moral questioning, towards the discovery and actualizing of previously unknown values, and they remain, keeping us focussed on the values we have made our own.

If these observations set us on the path towards self-discovery, there still remains a host of unanswered questions. The most prominent of these concern the character of moral knowledge itself. What does it mean to say that something is valuable, that something is right, that an action is good? What do we know when we know value? How do we know when we have attained such knowledge? It is to these questions that we turn in the next chapter. Our aim is to build upon the insights here and to carry forward the work of attending to our personal experiences of moral knowing. In the next phase of our inquiry, however, we encounter a dimension of moral experience which poses a distinct challenge to our method of self-discovery: the dimension of sociality.

## Chapter 2

# The Social Structure of Moral Knowledge

Have you ever been in a bank or a shop when it was robbed? Maybe your home was broken into, or you had your purse or wallet stolen on the street? Perhaps you were the clerk in the shop who had to face the robber's gun. Were you one of the people in the bank who had to lie down on the floor? Do you remember the terror? Were you tempted to do something heroic and possibly stupid? Or did you try to become invisible like I did? Surely you were struck by the difference between television and real life. This was not glamorous; it was ugly.

If your experience was anything like mine, it was horrible! More than this, your feelings of horror and indignation were rooted in something real. There is something terribly wrong in what the thieves did! Oh yes, you may have made something good out of the experience. Indeed, the event may have helped you get insights into social factors that lead to such crimes. These insights lend moral complexity to this episode in your life. Perhaps you wrestled with guilt feelings that you failed to do something to prevent or halt the crime. Maybe you even discovered that there were mitigating factors, that the event was not purely and simply a theft, but a more complex moral reality involving the thieves' efforts to help others in need. Yet in the middle of this complexity there remains a clear moral reality: there is something wrong about theft. You know this. We all know this.

If you have had an experience like this, you might have stopped to wonder about your moral knowledge. What sort of thing do you know, when you know that theft is wrong? What kind of thing is this moral knowledge? What are some of its features?[32] Moral knowledge

---

[32] This is the line of questioning which directs Lonergan's overall study of human knowing. Rather than questioning whether knowledge ever occurs, Lonergan accepts the fact that we sometimes achieve reliable knowledge and he asks about the features of the acts that yield this knowledge and the characteristics of the knowledge which is achieved. See, e.g., "Introduction," in *Insight*, 12–24.

is quite familiar and commonplace. We all have experiences of reliable moral knowledge. As long as we remain serious, particularly after instances like the theft, we do not doubt that theft really is wrong. We certainly wonder about how this knowledge figures into our total understanding of complex cases. But this does not change our basic moral knowledge about theft. Stealing is wrong. What sort of knowledge is this? How is it different from knowledge of facts? This will be the concern of this chapter.

To launch our inquiry, we will begin with a few observations about the theft experience. For the sake of clarity, we will proceed by making three sets of contrasts. Sometimes we think about ethics in images that are misleading. This happens frequently in all areas of life. For example, if we were trying to reflect on the lofty question, "What is human nature?" it would help to begin by observing that we humans are not the same as rocks; we are different from lettuce, and, despite some initial similarities we might observe in other people we know, we are very different from mice and chickens. Seeing these differences at the outset can prevent answers to later questions from slipping into absurdity.

To set the discussion moving in the right direction, we will begin with three observations about *what moral knowledge is not*. This will allow us to say something about *what it is*: moral knowledge is not a quality, but a direction of change; it is not about individual events, but about relations among events; and it is not about action in isolation, but about living with other people.

## Not a Quality, but a Direction of Change

One of the ways we might think about our experience of theft is to imagine that the event possesses the quality of "wrongness." The words "good," "bad," "right," and "wrong" are adjectives that modify nouns and they lead us to think that the theft possesses the quality of the adjective, in this case the quality of "badness" or "wrongness." Those of us who have read Robert Pirsig's *Zen and the Art of Motorcycle Maintenance*[33] remember his struggle to understand value as "quality."

Once we begin speaking about moral value as a quality, our imaginations take over. We are led to compare moral value with other

---

[33]    Robert M. Pirsig, *Zen and the Art of Motorcycle Maintenance: An Inquiry into Values* (Toronto, New York: Bantam Books, 1974).

qualities, like colour, texture, and taste. Then we ask where this quality comes from, how it adheres to things, and how it imbues things with its characteristic features. We imagine moral value as a paint that we might spread over things. Once the image takes hold, the inquiry is set in motion, generating its own questions, supplying its own data, and directing the inquiry in accordance with the analogy.

Moral value is not a quality! A better image to direct our inquiry than that of a substance like paint, applied to things, is the notion of a direction of change. A direction invokes the image of motion or change, and expresses a relation between where this change comes from and where it is going. Similarly, moral knowledge does not grasp the facts or features of a static situation; it grasps a dynamism, the motion of a series of events which are set into play by a decision to act.[34] We may use the words "good" or "bad" to describe a sunset or the behaviour of our dog, but we are not using these terms in the moral sense. When we speak of moral "rightness" or "goodness," we mean human action and the direction of events which unfolds from this action.[35]

Our moral knowledge of theft is knowledge about this motion, from its conditions of origin through to its impacts and goals. Theft shifts the trajectory of human affairs. It erupts out of conditions of ignorance, malice, or despair and leaves our lives with debris to clean up, wounds to be healed, and scars to be borne. When widespread, it makes many forms of government and commerce impossible. Even when theft appears "victimless," we know that in complex ways, the direction of present or future lives would be profoundly altered were we to pronounce it morally acceptable. Our knowledge of the moral character of theft is knowledge about this trajectory. To say that theft is wrong is to say that it erodes stability or progress and induces

---

[34] For a fuller discussion, see Lonergan, *Topics in Education*, 27–33, particularly 32–33.

[35] As was indicated in the first chapter, I make no distinction between the meanings of the terms *right* and *good*. Neither do I make any distinction between the terms *ethical* and *moral*. This is not to say that such distinctions have no merit. Rather, it is because these distinctions are often rooted in more advanced debates among alternative moral theories, and, consequently, are beyond the scope of what can be dealt with in this introductory presentation. For an example of an author for whom the distinction between *right* and *good* is important, see Rawls, *A Theory of Justice*, 446–452.

decline. All of this language expresses a direction of change inititiated by human action.

## Not about Individual Events, but about Relations among Events

When we try to determine whether theft is right or wrong, we find ourselves analyzing our moral experiences and assessing the relations among the elements. The event occurred in a situation or *context*. If the robbery was in a bank, we know that the money was customers' money being held in trust by the bankers, and this institutional scheme establishes clear lines of entitlement. The money did not belong to the thief. Moral knowledge expresses something about these contexts, but it also says something about *intentions*. If the thief were stealing to help others in real need, the event becomes morally more complex. The event might still involve a theft, but it would now be more than simply a theft. This is different than if he or she stole for personal gain. Our moral knowledge of theft says something about the thief's intentions.

Furthermore, our moral knowledge says something about the *consequences* of actions. Victims suffer losses that can involve traumatic changes to their lives. Stealing alters the direction of people's participation in property transactions because it erodes confidence and instills fear. It also changes the thief's own habits of valuing. Finally, quite apart from personal or immediately foreseeable consequences, actions usually form part of larger *structures of social action* which have their own *goals* or objectives. Our knowledge about theft presumes a basic fairness to the overall financial system. Theft violates this fairness. If financial institutions themselves become radically corrupt, then seizing the property of others can take on a completely different moral meaning. Such is the case when corrupt tyrants are overthrown and their assets impounded. Moral knowledge concerns all of these elements.

Moral knowledge is not knowledge of any of these elements in isolation. It is a grasp of the *relations* among all of these elements of moral experience.[36] It is true that we speak of good actions, good

---

[36] For a discussion of a more traditional Roman Catholic approach to understanding the relations among acts, intentions, and circumstances, see O'Connell, *Principles for a Catholic Morality* 196–200.

social structures, bad intentions, and evil consequences, but these expressions imply a relation between actions and their contexts, between intentions on the one hand, and consequences and goals on the other, and among social structures, the objectives they achieve, and the obligations they place on individual citizens. When we know that stealing is wrong, we know that in contexts of social structures where property fairly belongs to others, the action of taking this property for the goal of personal gain causes a deterioration in human living. What we know about this relation is that the overall trajectory of the scheme of events is one of decline rather than progress or stability. *Moral knowledge is knowledge of the trajectory of progress or decline that is expressed in the movement from a situation, through intentions and social structures, to action directed towards goals, and actual consequences.*

Of course, to know that theft is wrong does not imply that we know whether a particular case qualifies as an instance of theft. To know this, we must move beyond knowledge of the rule to attain knowledge of the particular case. This might require knowing a lot more than the morality of theft. Still, we do know something when we know the rule. What we know is that when a case reveals the trajectory of decline expressed by theft, it really is wrong.

Moral knowledge is knowledge of these relations; it is relational. This is not to say, however, that ethical knowledge is merely "relative." The terms "relative" and "relativism" when applied to ethics mean something else. Ethical relativism is usually the claim that when two people from different perspectives or cultures try to understand the same moral situation, they will attain different results and that these differences cannot be reconciled within a common evaluative framework.[37] We are not saying this. How could we? Those who write books or try to convince others of something cannot be relativists. If they were, they would realize from the outset that the attempt to convince another is a contradiction.

A good analogy for what is meant by "relational" is the law of physics which says that, all things being equal, falling objects accelerate at the rate of 32 feet per second per second. Physicists know that this law expresses the fact that all objects near the surface of the earth will

---

[37] Ninian Smart presents an introduction to this discussion in "Relativism in Ethics," in James Childress and John Macquarrie, eds., *The Westminster Dictionary of Christian Ethics* (Philadelphia: Westminster Press, 1986) 531–32.

pick up speed as they fall and (barring the effects of friction from air resistance) their speed will increase by 32 feet per second every second that they are falling. This law tells us nothing about what object is falling, how high it is, or how long it has been falling. It does not tell us anything about how fast the object was travelling initially. Furthermore, it does not even tell us anything about how quickly the object will accelerate in actuality, because it admits that air friction plays a role in slowing things down and that other forces could also exert an influence. What this law does describe is a relation between the speed of a falling object at one point in its fall and its speed at another point in its fall, granted a given proximity to earth and the absence of other intervening factors.

Is the knowledge expressed by this law objective? Yes, as long as we understand that the term "objective" does not require the law to say everything about everything, or even everything about anything. The knowledge is objective, but it is still relational because what is objective is the truth of the relation. So it is with our moral knowledge. Knowing that theft is wrong is knowing that the relation among the elements that make up theft will remain valid even when the outcome is influenced by other factors not expressed in the moral law.[38]

Moral knowledge can express something objective, permanent and true about things and still be relational. This does not imply that all moral knowledge is actually objective. Much of it is not. Even when we find that it is, we usually discover that it is incomplete and even, at times, irrelevant. Yet when moral knowledge is correct, what is objectively valid are relations among the various elements of moral experience. What is expressed by moral knowledge is a relation of progress or decline in the motion from context and social structures, through intention and action, to the goals and consequences that they intend and achieve.

---

[38] There have been numerous debates around the issues of "objectivity" and "relativity" in ethics in the past twenty-five years. For an introduction to some of these debates see the essays in Charles Curran and Richard McCormick, eds. *Readings in Moral Theology, No. 1: Moral Norms and Catholic Tradition* (New York: Paulist Press, 1979). For discussions of some of the issues in the debates, see, e.g., Kenneth R. Melchin, "Revisionists, Deontologists, and the Structure of Moral Understanding," *Theological Studies* 51 (1991): 389–416; and John Mahoney, "The Challenge of Moral Distinctions," *Theological Studies* 53 (1992): 663–682.

### Not about Action in Isolation, but about Living with Other People

Let us make one final clarification by contrast. Many of us were taught that the central issue in ethics was integrity or duty. The ultimate sin was giving in to the pressure to conform to the dictates of society. Acting responsibly meant refusing society, it meant acting according to our consciences, living up to our convictions regardless of whether this put us at odds with others.

This aspect of personal decision-making is doubtless important to ethical knowledge and action. Still, if living out our moral knowledge requires going against society, this does not mean that our moral knowledge is anti-social. Quite the contrary. Our principles themselves, unless they are totally absurd, envision new forms of *living with other people*. If moral obligations or rights remain in force regardless of their apparent consequences for others, this is so because of other, more fundamental dimensions of social, historical living that they aim to preserve and promote.

This is clear in the case of theft. If theft is rampant in society, our moral stance may require us to go against the crowd, to stand up and be true to ourselves in the face of public censure. However, our moral knowledge itself, our knowledge that theft is wrong, aims at restoring a new and more wholesome way of living with others. It aims at renewing relations based upon trust and trustworthiness. It affirms that these relations open doors to rich and diverse forms of human flourishing.

Moral knowledge is about living with other people. Historically, ethical reflection arose as a response to problems in social living which could not be resolved with the tools at hand. The great ethical controversies were debates about problems which were straining the fabric of social life and threatening social breakdown.[39] The perennial calls for moral renewal tended to be counter-cultural and thus appeared to be anti-social. Yet reformers intended to reverse major social decline and renew society. For people from all quarters to live together requires the greatest vigilance, the closest attention to the forms of our living.

---

[39] John Noonan presents a number of excellent studies of this process of historical development in ethics. See, e.g., John T. Noonan, Jr., *Contraception*, enlarged ed. (Cambridge, MA: Harvard University Press, 1986; orig. 1965); *The Scholastic Analysis of Usury* (Cambridge, MA: Harvard University Press, 1957); and "Development in Moral Doctrine," *Theological Studies* 54 (1993): 662–677.

This attention is the work of ethics, and its results are the strategies for the most comprehensive and durable forms of living with other people.

### Three Meanings of the Word "Good"

So much for our clarifications by contrast. The next step involves observing something odd about our own moral language. Quite apart from differences among people's actual views on right and wrong in situations, there seem to be more fundamental structural differences in the way we think about *good* and *bad, right* and *wrong.* Furthermore, if we observe our own language and thinking over the course of a few days and weeks, we find that we all shift back-and-forth among three quite different meanings of the word "good."[40]

In some cases, "good" seems to mean little more than something that satisfies an individual desire or a personal interest. In other cases "good" seems to imply an accountability to a wider social order that transcends personal desire. In still other cases, invoking "the good" seems to call for a critical evaluation of social orders within wider, more universal horizons of historical progress or decline. What is going on here?

These three meanings for "good" arise because there are three levels or horizons of meaning on which ethical questions can be raised and answered. The *first* is the level of personal interest or desire. We are often carried into action or into deliberation about action because of personal desires. When problems can be handled on this level without further complication, the terms "good" and "bad," "right" and "wrong" mean little more than that actions or events respond adequately to personal desires and interests. It is not difficult to think of instances of this. When we act to protect ourselves from harm, to feed ourselves, or to rest after an exhausting day, the "good" that we seek involves little more than the satisfaction of personal desire. Sometimes issues arise that involve nothing of significance beyond this first level of moral meaning.

---

40  Bernard Lonergan presents the three levels of the good in *Insight*, Chapter 18.1.1; and *Topics in Education*, 33–38. For a discussion of the links between Lonergan's ethical theory and the stage theory of Lawrence Kohlberg, see Walter Conn, *Conscience*; and "Moral Development: Is Conversion Necessary?" in Matthew Lamb, ed., *Creativity and Method* (Milwaukee, Wisc.: Marquette University Press, 1981) 307–324.

Often this is not so, however. Most moral deliberations involve considerations beyond personal desire, and problems are revealed as ethical because our personal desires conflict with the desires of others or with concerns that cannot be reduced simply to desire. In fact, as we saw in the previous chapter, there are different types of desires even in our individual lives. Some of these are not merely personal; they intend the welfare of others. This is not to say that personal desires become unimportant. Our desires for personal health and safety, for some measure of fulfillment, for satisfaction in our jobs, for some measure of physical comfort, remain important aspirations in life. They are often the desires that propel us into action and, in many cases, they remain significant in the process of moral evaluation. In most cases, however, we need to move beyond this first horizon of ethical meaning so that we can make a judgement between conflicting desires within a higher frame of reference. This is because we live with other people.

In our actions and deliberations we usually encounter the desires and interests of others. When their desires and interests conflict with ours, it is often because they reveal our complex involvements in cooperative projects. At this point, a *second*, more comprehensive meaning of the word "good" comes into play. When we use the words "good" or "right" to say that we were treated honestly in a business dealing, or that a friend's support helped us through a difficult time, the word expresses something, not just about our desires or about these particular situations, but about their links with wider patterns of relations that constitute our business and social lives. In these cases, "good" reflects an awareness of interpersonal order or social structure. It expresses our understanding that these actions fit in with or promote a range of social orders that sustain our communal living. It implies that they nurture the relationships that bind people together in cooperative living to achieve what none could achieve on their own.

Certainly, a fully theoretical analysis of the social structures implicated in our moral actions would be very complex and our day-to-day moral deliberations do not take us into such explicit analyses. Yet our daily deliberations do appeal to tried and true notions, to moral maxims that express insights into social order and have proven themselves over time. Common-sense notions like courtesy and respect for others describe ways of behaving that smooth the many encounters between citizens in the routines of city life. Rules against lying and stealing prohibit ways of acting that would cripple the routines of business and the economy. Things like understanding and fidelity nourish the relationships of family life which are so important for the development of young children.

Throughout history, sages, elders, philosophers, theologians, social scientists, artists, and journalists have subjected such maxims to considerable scrutiny. They have reflected on patterns of social living through the ages and have pondered over them. When we think about specific ethical issues, we may not engage directly in social analysis, but we often appeal to the results of such analyses as summed up in the common-sense wisdom of the ages.

The *third* level of meaning of moral language comes into play when we realize that our social structures themselves may be in decline. In this case, to speak of "fitting in" with such structures may mean being co-opted, it may mean playing into the hands of power brokers or interest groups, it may mean evading or refusing a wider responsibility to correct, to transform, or to rebuild patterns of social living. At this third level of meaning we are aware of victimization and oppression, and we see the dark side of social structures within wider historical frames of reference. We may remember patterns of living in which justice or generosity was more fully realized, or we may envision such patterns as future possibilities.

These wider horizons reveal to us the longer dynamics of historical progress and decline. The third level of ethical deliberation arises when we ask, not simply whether our actions fit into social structures, but whether the structures themselves are "good." On this level, we evaluate our social structures against wider standards, but we do so, not by constructing abstract scales or pure models, but by getting hosts of concrete insights into instances of progress and decline within historical living and within the ecologies which are our home. Such occasions of insight include moments when we discover that our notions of justice have excluded women and people of colour; moments when we discover the need for institutions to resolve international disputes; moments when we discover that patterns of economic "order" threaten the global environment.

When we criticize social structures, we discern vectors of decline and deterioration that they bring about and that new actions and structures are called to reverse. Conversely, when we find social structures to be "good," it is because we have discerned vectors of progress and enhancement on a broader scale which should follow when such structures are allowed to emerge and thrive. Ethical language on the third level of moral meaning refers to these longer ranging historical vectors. These vectors and their implied patterns of action are the stuff of the great epics and religious narratives of history.

What is interesting about the different meanings of the word "good" on these three levels is that they each imply a different attitude towards social structures. On the first level, we may be aware of our relations with others, we may have some understanding of social institutions, structures, and systems, but our ethical attitude is governed by an interesting twist on this knowledge. Here, our focus is not on the social structures; it is on our personal desires. Here, personal desire rules. On this first level, in fact, social structures often become mere instruments or means for the fulfillment of personal desire.

This is precisely what changes when we move to the second level of moral meaning. Here, social structure is valued in its own right. When conflicts arise between merely personal interest and social obligation, social obligation prevails. The reasons for this hierarchy are quite complex, and some of these reasons will be explored further in this and later chapters. What is important here, however, is to note the difference in ethical attitude. When I move into this second level, I see something I had not seen before: the awareness that "we are all in this together." I recognize interdependence, collegiality, and an intrinsic worth in the collaboration itself. I begin to understand that I need the cooperation of others for the fulfillment of my desires. That is not all: I see that the same holds true for you, and for others, and that this will continue to be so. This generalized insight involves some measure of identification with others, empathy with others, solidarity with others. Here, the social orders that unite us in common projects reign as the predominant values.

On the third level, social orders become the object of radical scrutiny. At this point our ethical attitude towards structures and institutions is critical. The question is, Are they agents of progress or of decline? Notice again that the intent of this scrutiny is not to abolish social order, but to renew or transform it. By evaluating social structures against the wider horizons of history, we discern the vectors of progress and decline that will be the tools for this work of correction and

46

renewal. In an important sense, this third level of ethical meaning maintains a concern for social structure, but we begin now to understand structure dynamically. Consequently we take up this concern for structure into a more comprehensive evaluative framework that is governed by dynamic norms of development, flourishing, liberation, and transcendence.

One final note: the three levels or horizons of moral meaning are not simply three alternative ways of viewing. They cannot be understood by an analogy to visual perspective, nor can they be reduced to mere cultural differences: they are clearly hierarchical. The movement from the first, through the second, to the third represents a real advance in our capacity to evaluate morally or ethically, because each higher level is more comprehensive than the lower. If deliberation on the lower level is governed by a narrower commitment to specific interests or specific social structures, deliberation on the higher levels allows a wider range of commitments and concerns into the picture. Evaluation on the higher levels asks about the relationships among these concerns and refuses to stop short of a more comprehensive understanding that does justice to them all.

To say that the three levels of moral meaning are hierarchical does not mean that all issues in life must be evaluated on the third level. The fact is that many issues involve little more than personal desire or interest. Others can and should be settled within the framework of social structures as they are. What it does mean, however, is that if we want to make decisions in a morally mature way, we must be able to think and act on all three levels. This is so because we can judge the appropriateness of a decision on a lower level only from the perspective of the higher. Growth towards moral maturity entails movement through the levels, and this includes learning which level of analysis is appropriate for different issues. Further, our desires and our insights into social structures undergo subtle transformations throughout life as we mature ethically.

## What Is a "Social Structure"?

If moral meaning functions on three levels and if the levels reveal distinctly different attitudes towards social structures, then it might help to have some idea of what a "social structure" is. This question has been the object of considerable study by many philosophers, sociologists, political scientists and theologians.[41] Some preliminary insights can help guide our thinking in this area.

While the term "social" suggests an aggregate or quantity of individual persons, the term "structure" signals that what we are seeking to understand will not be achieved through a quantitative summation or calculus.[42] Many of us have been encouraged to think about society by analogy to opinion polls or elections, in which outcomes are the result of summations of individual decisions or opinions. The fact is that most social living does not work this way. Families, schools, businesses, prisons, marketplaces, governments, clubs, voluntary associations, friendships, cities, and civilizations involve ordered patterns of actions and relationships. While many of these structures have been invented by people and spelled out in charters or constitutions, many others have emerged spontaneously. If a social structure is not an aggregate or summation, then what is it?

Like all structures, social structures involve elements and linkages. Unlike others, however, they involve *meaning* — words, and gestures, and all of the mental acts that lie behind outward events. In some way or another, social structures involve sets of linkages among acts of meaning.[43] Some preliminary insights into social structures can be

---

41  Anthony Giddens presents an introductory discussion of social structures within sociology in *New Rules of Sociological Method* (London: Hutchinson, 1976) 118–26. For an introduction to the way in which the analysis of social structures has influenced liberation theology, see Gustavo Gutiérrez, *A Theology of Liberation*, trans. C. Inda and J. Eagleson (Maryknoll, N.Y.: Orbis Books, 1973); *We Drink from Our Own Wells*, trans. M. J. O'Connell (Maryknoll, N.Y.: Orbis Books, 1984). For a discussion of how sin and evil are understood in terms of social structures, see Mark O'Keefe, *What Are They Saying About Social Sin?* (N.Y.: Paulist Press, 1990).

42  This distinction between understanding society as an aggregate of individual actions or as a structure is brought out by John Langan in "Common Good," in *The Westminster Dictionary of Christian Ethics*, 102. See also the articles by David Hollenbach, "Common Good," in *The New Dictionary of Catholic Social Thought*, 192–97; and "The Common Good Revisited," *Theological Studies* 50 (1989): 70–94.

43  For a series of analyses of social structures that draw upon Lonergan's understanding of linked sets of operations of meaning, see Kenneth R. Melchin, "Pluralism, Conflict, and the Structure of the Public Good," in M. Lalonde, ed., *The Promise of Critical Theology* (Waterloo, ON: Wilfrid Laurier University Press, 1995) 75–92; "Moral Knowledge and the Structure of Cooperative Living," *Theological Studies* 52 (1992): 495–523; "Military and Deterrence Strategy and the 'Dialectic of Community'," in T. Fallon and P. B. Riley, eds., *Religion and Culture* (Albany, N.Y.: State University of New York Press, 1987) 293–309.

gained by looking at a simple conversation. And, to better illustrate how social structures unfold and the role they play on the three levels of moral meaning, we will examine a specific type of conversation, a consumer purchase transaction.[44]

Consider a simple transaction. A customer enters a computer store, browses through the merchandise, is approached by the merchant, describes his or her needs, and asks advice on what system best suits these needs within a price range. The merchant offers information on the various products, indicates prices, and makes a few recommendations. The customer asks further questions about products and begins the process of negotiating prices. Negotiations go forward until an agreement is reached, the customer expresses an intention to purchase, the appropriate bills of sale are printed, payment is secured, the merchandise is packaged and handed over, and the customer leaves the store with an exchange of regards.

A huge number of transactions like this occur every day. Their levels of complexity vary: some involve more elaborate consultation and negotiation, while others require little more than a nod to a checkout clerk to ratify the contract to purchase.

In what sense is this a "social structure"? How can an understanding of this transaction help us understand moral value? To answer this question we must break the transaction into its elements and understand the links between the elements which make it function time and again as a structure or scheme. The key to a structure is not that it occurs once, but that it recurs time and again, at least in certain environments. The stability of the structure is secured, not by outward factors, but by the internal linkages among the elements.[45]

The first of these elements can be called the entry or the opening stage. Customers enter shops with standard sets of desires and expectations. When they are greeted (or perhaps merely tolerated) by a merchant, these expectations are confirmed in a subtle but significant

44  The following sketch was originally presented in Kenneth R. Melchin, "Economies, Ethics, and the Structure of Social Living," *Humanomics* 10 (1994): 21–57. This article presents three examples of the way structures of social meaning operate in economic life to shape moral obligation and action.

45  I am drawing here on Lonergan's concept of "recurrence schemes." See *Insight*, Chapter 4.2; McShane, *Randomness, Statistics and Emergence*, 206–229; Melchin, *History, Ethics, and Emergent Probability*, 181–87.

exchange of gestures and responses.[46] This validation process can have quite a number of elements or it can be quite simple. People who own an array of computers and wish to place them on display for sale must declare their intentions to the public in some way or another (by a sign outside, an advertisement in the newspaper, a listing in the phone book, and so forth). Similarly, people who wish to buy (rather than steal or smash) computers must declare their intentions in some way to shop owners. What both parties need is some assurance that their expectations are shared.

In many cases one person will nod or say a word in response to the other's gesture, and thus will acknowledge shared meaning and validate the business relationship. Each party must take the role of the other, anticipate the other's response to a gesture, and watch for confirmation, in order for this validation to succeed. When this role-taking goes according to expectations, it is almost totally pre-conscious, practically invisible. It becomes conspicuous when expectations are found to be mistaken. Generally, the behaviour of customers and merchants follows custom or convention. Yet one way or another, this conventional discourse requires that complementary expectations be communicated, that participants engage in some minimal role-taking, and that expectations be confirmed by the response of the other.[47] The suspicion that results when any of these elements is absent is often enough to put an end to further discussion or to set in motion complex responses to enforce or reinforce security.

The next step might be called the negotiation stage. It involves a mutual exchange in which the parties determine the customer's needs, the merchant's products, and the relative compatibility of the two. Like the first step, this stage of the transaction has a goal. For the parties to proceed to the following stage, they must find a compatibility or a "fit" among the needs, products, and prices. With a computer

---

[46] This analysis of the scheme in terms of gesture, response, and role-taking draws upon the work of Gibson Winter, particularly his analysis of George Herbert Mead. See Winter, *Elements for a Social Ethic* (New York: Macmillan, 1966); George Herbert Mead, *On Social Psychology*, edited by Anselm Strauss (Chicago: University of Chicago Press, 1964). See also Melchin, "Moral Knowledge," 509–515.

[47] In large supermarkets or department stores this confirmation of intended meaning is ensured, in part, by security guards who watch customers looking for signs of duplicity of intent, by signs informing customers that this is going on, and by the fact that we all know this.

purchase, this can involve extended discussion of the details of computer technology. Just as often, however, the success of this stage depends on the relative compatibility of the styles of the participants. The exchange of gestures and words can vary depending on the personalities, the cultural backgrounds, or the professional formations of the participants. One way or another, these styles must also "fit" for the parties to come to an agreement to proceed. Many potentially viable transactions are broken off because a salesperson is too aggressive, a customer too demanding, a merchant seems indifferent, or a consumer shows too little interest.

This second stage of the transaction, the negotiation stage, can begin only when the first stage has succeeded in establishing a context of shared expectations or meaning. Merchants who are suspicious of a customer's intentions might proceed to do business, but without giving themselves fully over to the dynamics of the next stage. Consequently, the opening stage tends to function as a condition of possibility for the second stage. In a similar way, the successful achievement of the goals of the negotiation puts the last link in place for the transaction to continue on to the third stage. This is the stage of the contracting and the exchange of currency, bills of purchase, and merchandise. The outward form of this contracting involves familiar words, documents, and gestures.

"So have you decided to buy this system as described?"
"Yes!"
"Are you willing to sell it to me for this amount?"
"Yes!"
"Here's the money."
"Here's your receipt."
"Here's the computer."

What is interesting about this stage is its hidden complexity, its fragility, and its awesome significance for the maintenance of civilization. The answer "Yes!" in each case involves far more than an outward gesture. Prior to the gesture there occurs an inner act, a commitment to the other to perform the outer act, a committing of oneself to a type of cooperation with another person that will have social consequences on which they can rely. This committing or promising is not a knowing in the sense of hitting on an insight or judging a course of action, but it is still an act of meaning, a rational act, an act involving the cognitional functions. It is a responsible decision which orients the self in relation to another person in accordance with some intelligible content that had been worked out in the previous stage.[48] The "Yes!" is not yet the acting, nor is it the process of determining how we will act, but it is the pivot between the two, the preparation to act in regard to the other, with the assurance that we will indeed follow through on our commitment.

When both parties pronounce their "Yes!", the contracting is done. Acting out the commitment involves the transfer of money, documents, and merchandise in accordance with this contracting. Yet it is the contracting that grounds the confidence that the exchange will proceed according to agreement. Even when some time separates the payment from the receipt of merchandise, we proceed in confidence. To some degree we have this confidence because we know that the courts and the police can be called in for enforcement. Still, anyone who has had to go this route knows that enforcement often involves personal demands that far exceed the value of the merchandise (and often with dubious results). For the most part, confidence is rooted, not in the assurance of enforcement, but in *the reciprocal attribution of a commitment to responsibility between the parties in the contracting*. This central moment in a transaction is a profoundly moral act; it is a mutual commitment to responsibility on the part of the participants in the transaction. As we shall see, it is by no means the only moral aspect of the scheme. Common-sense images of contracting, however, often obscure the profoundly moral thrust of this event.

While the contracting is the central act in the transaction, it is not the last event. The scheme is completed only when the two parties exchange parting gestures, the customer leaves the store, and the merchant sets his or her attention in readiness to receive the next customer. This may seem like a trivial aspect of the scheme, but this final closure represents the condition of possibility for the transaction scheme to begin again, for the merchant to deal with another customer, for the consumer to move on to another store. The economic significance of the transaction is not that it occurs once. Rather,

---

[48] Lonergan understands responsibility as a level of operation of a moral subject which directs a range of operations and skills towards a distinctive goal, the goal of authentic action. For more developed discussions, see Lonergan, *Method*, Chapters 1 and 2; Melchin, "Ethics in *Insight*"; Byrne, "Consciousness: Levels, Sublations, and the Subject as Subject"; and Vertin, "Judgments of Value."

purchases are economically significant because they recur in large numbers and in great diversity. It is the chain of transactions that takes goods and services from the earliest production stages to the market place and into our living. It is the volume of purchases that ensures the financial viability of merchants. And it is the diversity of goods and services, available in large enough numbers to serve us all, that is our "standard of living." For such volumes and diversity to flourish, it is necessary that each transaction scheme end in such a way that another can begin. Generally, this may require nothing more than a customer leaving the store, but if a transaction results in a shattering of confidence, the possibility for recurrence may depend on some form of healing. Furthermore, if confidence is shattered too frequently, on too wide a scale, the social measures for assuring recurrence may become significantly more complex and costly.

In its overall structure, the scheme involves four linked stages of acts of meaning, each fulfilling the condition for the next, and the last fulfilling the condition for another scheme to begin. For the needs or requirements of each party to be met, all four stages must occur in one form or another. At each stage we find a reciprocal exchange of meaning, a set of operations involving gestures, responses, and role-taking undertaken to confirm shared meaning. The transaction is a cooperative scheme involving the two parties' reciprocal contributions towards the achievement of mutual goals which neither could have achieved on their own. And while this scheme has a distinct internal structure and an identity of its own, it functions within a wider series of meaning schemes which, together, make up an economy and a society.

### Social Structures, Moral Obligations, and the Three Levels of Moral Meaning

Three things become clear from this analysis of the consumer purchase: (i) the scheme has an *internal structure* of stages which is identifiable because it remains relatively stable in hosts of different contexts; (ii) the scheme has a range of *goals or objectives* which can be met only if the participants move successfully through this internal structure of stages; (iii) this structure imposes a range of *moral obligations* that the participants must fulfill if they are to move successfully through the stages to achieve their goals.[49]

(i) While the outward features of the discourse in a transaction can vary widely from one context to another, there remains a basic form to each scheme which arises not from the cultural context per se but from the *internal structure* of the process. This is so because the scheme has stages and each stage builds upon the previous to move the participants towards their goals. Whatever anybody says in the opening stage, it must satisfy both parties of the mutuality of intent. However they manage the negotiation, the participants must come to some agreement before the money and the goods change hands. The requirements of the scheme can be fulfilled in a variety of ways, but the central elements and links must still be present.[50]

(ii) There is a difference between the *goals of the scheme* and what the participants would say they want. The goals of the scheme are defined by its internal structure, by the fact that participants must move through this structure to achieve their personal objectives, and by the role that the scheme plays in the wider ecologies of economy and society. Participants may want individual things out of purchase transactions, but if they are to attain them, they must follow the internal logic of the scheme and fulfill its structural requirements. If a next stage is to begin, then the obligations of the former stage must be met. If the customer wants his computer, then he must complete the whole scheme. If the merchant wants her income, then she must complete the transaction. Furthermore, if purchase transactions are to play their role in the overall economy, the goals of the scheme must be met in a fashion which builds and sustains customer confidence in the safety and the value of continued participation. For transactions to proliferate, these structural goals must be met, even when they conflict with individual desires.

---

[49] For a discussion of the way in which social schemes make demands and obligations on participants, see Byrne, "Jane Jacobs."

[50] For a similar type of analysis of the way in which "justice" needs to be understood in terms of the various "spheres" of social life, see Michael Walzer, *Spheres of Justice* (New York: Basic Books, 1983).

(iii) The obligations imposed on the participants by the structure of the scheme include *moral obligations*. The meaning and moral force of these obligations become clear when we understand how they facilitate the movement through the structure of the scheme. Social structures make it possible for people to join forces to accomplish together what none could achieve on their own, but they do so by making moral demands on their participants. For the negotiation stage to begin in earnest, both parties must be assured of the other's intention at the initial stage. This calls for some measure of openness and honesty. For the contracting stage to begin, the parties must together meet all of the technical, cultural, and inter-personal requirements of the negotiation stage. This can demand competence, sensitivity, consideration for others, and, at times, even generosity. For the closing stage to begin, the contracting must be declared and duly recorded. This most certainly requires a certain measure of integrity. And for other schemes of this type to begin again, the parties must leave the transaction secure in the knowledge that the real physical, psychological, legal, and financial hazards of doing business are not so overwhelming as to discourage any further participation in the marketplace. These moral obligations are real, and they are not trivial. In many periods of history, in many societies, or in many quarters of our own society, these obligations are not easily or frequently met by the ordinary citizen.[51]

At this point, the reader may object that this analysis seems to explain something about the social character of moral obligations, but it also seems to devalue these obligations. On the face of it, this analysis seems to suggest that moral obligations are merely means or instruments for the attainment of individual or personal desires. If moral obligations are rooted in social structures, and if social structures are the means for attaining what I want, then it would seem that moral obligations have no intrinsic worth, no value in their own right,

---

[51] For a discussion of how trade schemes function differently in other socio-religious contexts, see Karl Polanyi, Conrad M. Arensberg, and Harry W. Pearson, eds., *Trade and Market in the Early Empires* (Chicago: Henry Regnery Company/Gateway Ed., 1971; orig. 1957). An analysis of one of these schemes is presented in Melchin, "Economies," 33–39.

but are merely instruments for self-satisfaction. What seems to reign supreme in this analysis is individual desire.[52] What is going on here?

To answer this objection requires recalling that moral understanding can go forward on three levels of meaning, the level of individual desire, the level of social order, and the level of historical progress and decline. Each level of meaning involves a distinctive ethical attitude towards social structures. This attitude stamps its distinctive character upon the obligations imposed by the schemes. Furthermore, this attitude changes the moral form of our participation in the schemes. The objection formulated above presupposes the first level of moral meaning, where personal desire reigns supreme and social structures are a means to this fulfillment. This first level, however, does not pronounce the final word on moral obligations. And it is interesting to observe how the moral character of our involvement shifts as we participate in social life with a commitment to the three levels.

In some cases, a transaction can succeed when participants are governed only by the *first* level of moral meaning, the level of personal desire. Both parties, then, view the transaction only as a way to fulfilling their personal desires. If either party, however, foregoes or violates one of the internal requirements for personal advantage, then the scheme may be derailed or distorted. When this happens, the exploited party often comes to discover the exploitation, and this will affect his or her next involvement. When this recurs often enough in culture, commerce becomes radically distorted or ambiguous.

It may be that parties come to understand this general disruption which comes with widespread exploitation and accept the obligations of the scheme only as a means for securing their self-interest. Then problems will arise only when they can get what they want with relative impunity. This will be common, however, for complex social schemes will forever present abundant opportunities for innovative forms of exploitation, and the beleaguered institutions of law enforcement will invariably trail behind the innovators. When the fundamental commitment to self-interest prevails over all else, society

---

[52] The general thrust of this criticism is presented by John Finnis in *Fundamentals of Ethics* (Washington, D.C.: Georgetown University Press, 1983) 42–50. For a response to Finnis' claim that this amounts to a criticism of Lonergan's ethics, see Joseph Cassidy, "Extending Bernard Lonergan's Ethics."

is faced with the problem that short-term personal rewards are purchased at the cost of longer-ranging public order.

What is clear is that the complex social structures of civilizations lead a fragile existence in cultures governed by the first level of moral meaning. To nurture stable social schemes over the long haul requires that citizens cultivate the habits and virtues for regularly living up to the moral obligations imposed by the schemes. This is the work of generations. For this to occur, there must be a wide-scale commitment to social order, not simply as a means to an end, but as a value in its own right.

This is what occurs when structures are governed by the *second* level of moral meaning, the commitment to social order. Here, vast ranges of such schemes can function with awesome regularity. This regularity is rooted, in part, in the fact that transactions are completed without complication, because people come to know their obligations and are committed to fulfilling them. It is also rooted in the fact that the commitment to order permits complications and breakdowns to be repaired or redressed when they do occur. The good of order is maintenance of what is: social orders are enjoyed, appreciated, and nurtured for their own sake, in much the same way that an art or craft is loved and appreciated by its devotees.

When citizens participate in society on the second level of moral meaning, the relation between individual desire and social structure changes dramatically. Social schemes continue to function as conditions for the attainment of desires, but this is no longer understood as a relation of means to ends. Instead, citizens come to understand their welfare as implicated in the wider fabric of social relations. Concern for personal welfare becomes inseparable from this wider social concern and, gradually, as this understanding becomes habitual, the calculation of individual benefits gives way to a sustained preoccupation with social order.[53]

---

[53] I would argue that the flurry of texts on the "common good" in the past ten years reflects this effort to elevate ethical discourse in politics and economics in North America from the first to the second level of moral meaning. See Herman Daly and John B. Cobb, Jr., *For the Common Good* (Boston: Beacon Press, 1989); Bill Jordan, *The Common Good* (Oxford: Basil Blackwell, 1989); David Hollenbach, "The Common Good Revisited"; Williams and Houck, eds., *The Common Good and U.S. Capitalism.* For works that move in this same direction but which do not explicitly use the expression "the common good," see Amitai Etzioni, *The Moral*

The second level of moral meaning can sustain social order, for it is a commitment to existing orders and obligations. For the same reason, however, those who are locked into the second level cannot easily tolerate significant alterations in the structure of social orders. Furthermore, if a scheme like the consumer purchase becomes implicated in a wider series of schemes whose overall dynamic is exploitative or destructive, those thinking on the second level will not recognize this easily. The diagnosis of the problem and the prescription for cure will require a move to the third level of moral meaning.

On the *third* level of moral meaning, citizens begin asking about the relations among extant orders and the relations to past and future orders. Here, we ask if our transactions sustain economies that are truly "good" for us. We begin to wonder about rising levels of unemployment, increasing economic difficulties experienced by marginalized groups, increasing burdens on governments as our demands exceed our willingness to pay, increasing reports of human misery as our economic schemes get exported to foreign lands. While the commitment to order is attuned to the obligations and requirements of maintaining social structures (the second level), the commitment to historical progress is attuned to changes in structures, particularly changes that affect human welfare.[54]

Quite frequently, the third level involves us in social critique. Those thinking and acting at this level, however, do not simply criticize: they are also committed to the values and obligations required for the renewal of these structures. The discernment of these values and how they are to be lived is neither clear nor simple, particularly in the early decades of renewal, but the values and obligations on the third level

---

*Dimension* (New York: The Free Press, 1989); Robert N. Bellah et al, *Habits of the Heart: Individualism and Commitment in American Life* (New York: Harper & Row / Perennial Library, 1986). See also the other texts listed in the "Selected Readings on Christian Ethics," at the end of this book. I am indebted to Jerome Miller for clarifying some of the issues here.

[54] I would suggest that this shift to the third level of moral meaning is what marks the recent directions in the work of the Catholic Bishops Conferences in the U.S. and Canada. See Sandra Yocum Mize, "National Conference of Catholic Bishops, United States," in *The New Dictionary of Catholic Social Thought*, 665–69; and Kenneth R. Melchin, "National Conference of Catholic Bishops, Canada," in *The New Dictionary of Catholic Social Thought*, 660–64. What distinguishes the third level is the concern for progressive transformations in social structures in the name of human welfare.

tend to tolerate a certain lack of concreteness or precision. Prior to working out concrete strategies for action, moral analysis asks more generally about directions of change, vectors for renewal, and possible goals that such renewal would seek to realize.

Moral action and deliberation on the third level of moral meaning has a distinctive *heuristic* thrust; it orients our moral inquiry in a specific direction, and animates it with a distinctive concern. It aims at realizing social structures which may, as yet, not exist in any significant measure. It is driven by a concern for order, but for an order which is in the making. Consequently, the values and obligations that animate reflection and action are less directly attached to concretely functioning schemes, and more generically aimed at future goods which such schemes must promote. These goods are, to some degree, understood as the correctives to extant evils. They are also open-ended, or imprecisely defined goods, informed by extrapolations from existing goods. We desire full participation in an economy for marginalized groups because we see the evils wrought by exclusion. Yet we also appreciate real gains experienced by current participants and wish them upon the marginalized. How these two go together is not entirely clear at the outset, but the twofold concern sets our inquiry in motion in a specific direction.

As historical efforts begin to succeed in effecting transformation and renewal in social structures, the obligations entailed in newly emerging structures begin to exert their obligatory force on their new participants. New forms of living call for new commitments, habits, and virtues. Thus, citizens are called to shift back to behaviour informed by the second level of moral meaning, the commitment to social order. Such participation, however, need not fall back into the limited horizons of second-level meaning. With care, discipline, and a commitment from all sectors of society, citizens can live in stable structures while still informed by the moral consciousness of third-level moral meaning.

To live like this, we have to accept a tension and ambiguity in moral life. This is so because diagnoses of social ills head in different directions when approached from the second and third levels of meaning. The commitment to order sees a problem as a failure in living up to the obligations entailed by order. The commitment to progress sees the problem as a failure in the order itself. Neither of these is automatically true. To ascertain the truth we must analyze concrete situations carefully, armed with questions and criteria from the two levels of moral meaning. This can take time and, in the interim, can take its toll on the patience of citizens. Yet if moral truth is what is sought, then the architects of public opinion need to create the climate of public patience required for this inquiry to go forward carefully and competently. There is no shortcut to moral understanding and judgement.

To live in stable structures with third-level moral consciousness, we must accept the complexities associated with the pursuit of moral knowledge. If they can endure the ambiguity associated with these complexities, citizens will enjoy the benefits of a corrective attention to deformations in social living while championing the values that humanize their lives. Given that societies are always in some degree of transition, we can expect that this multi-leveled moral discernment will be a permanent part of moral deliberation through the ages. What remains is for citizens to cultivate the virtues required, not only for operating on each level, but for shifting back and forth between them when the situation warrants.

## Summary

The objective of this chapter has been to introduce a way of thinking about the social character of moral knowledge. We drew upon a sample analysis of a consumer purchase to illustrate a rather novel approach to understanding social structures. This analysis brought to light some interesting insights into the way social structures impose moral obligations on their participants, but it also highlighted how these obligations are approached and lived differently on the three levels of moral meaning. Finally, a number of implications were suggested for those of us who must live in social structures in times of transition.

These reflections, of necessity, remain little more than a sketch, but they point in directions that can be promising for future ethical inquiry. Above all, my hope is that they make some sense for those who are serious about understanding their everyday moral experience. Our moral obligations do not fall wholesale from the sky. They emerge from people's efforts to order life in the interest of our most comprehensive notions of human well-being. This analysis has shown how a rather novel understanding of social structure can help us understand both the obligations entailed in this ordering and the well-being that it intends.

*Chapter 3*
# Moral Foundations and Moral Persons

I want to begin this chapter with a silly, but helpful picture of a society of citizens who, early in life, are called into some head office and issued ethical systems. At any point in the history of this society, there is an inventory, let us say, of five or six different ethical systems that are in vogue and have received the stamp of approval from head office. Each system is a logically coherent set of premises, arguments, conclusions, and rules that specify how the citizen will be required to act in particular situations. We can imagine that an Appendix would list reasonable paybacks to citizens, compensation for having to follow rules they do not like. But the official stamp of approval on the system assures citizens that these paybacks are fair, because the system has been decreed coherent. Since the society is democratic, citizens are allowed to make their own choices among the approved ethical systems. Of course, there are procedures for returns and exchanges in cases where citizens are dissatisfied. Once the ninety-day trial period is up, however, citizens are expected to live by their system of choice. Laws, police forces, and courts specify rules for respecting another's system (as long as it is approved), and there are penalties for violations of the laws of tolerance.

If you have ever taken an introductory course in ethics, you might have found yourself, in moments of distraction, conjuring up images like this. To be sure, your instructor did not have this silliness in mind. Yet your textbook might seem to suggest that a more sober version of this image is what ethics is really about. An introductory text typically presents a variety of moral theories, each proposing its own foundational principles. Philosophers and theologians from history are selected because of their high-profile impact on societies past and present.[55] Each theory seems to be a logically coherent system resting

---

[55]  See Edward Stevens, *Business Ethics* (New York: Paulist Press, 1979); Joseph Desjardins, *Environmental Ethics* (Belmont, CA: Wadsworth Publishing Company, 1993), Chapter 2.

on its first principles. Each theory seems to begin with its principles and develops by drawing out or deducing applications to everyday life. At times we are left with the impression that ethics is like shopping for a computer system: we pick our system and live with the consequences. While authors of introductory texts sometimes go to great pains to nuance or modify this portrayal, still, this image of a supermarket of logical systems often remains with us.

While this may seem an attractive way of presenting an introductory survey of moral theories, it is not a very helpful way of thinking about how moral knowing works in our lives. In most cases, it is not a helpful way of presenting the way that various thinkers themselves arrived at their theories. Most importantly, it presents a misleading impression about moral foundations.

It is true that ethicists through the ages have sought to formulate their insights into logically coherent theories and to identify foundations that apply to all areas of moral life. In most instances, however, they arrived at their foundational insights after years of struggling to understand particular issues that arose in concrete experience. Their concrete insights came first and their principles came later. Teachers often present ethical theories by beginning with general principles and working towards particular applications, while the ethicists themselves began with particular insights and worked towards general principles.[56]

Most importantly, this is also how we actually learn ethics in our lives, even when we are taught by others. Teaching and learning in ethics, when it is effective for living, is not the dispensing of logical principles from which we deduce concrete applications; rather, it is a

---

[56] For a discussion of this movement from concrete insights to general principles in the work of Kant, see Lewis White Beck, "Translator's Introduction," in Immanuel Kant, *Critique of Practical Reason* (Indianapolis: Bobbs-Merrill, 1956) vii–ix. For a discussion of the life and work of Aristotle leading up to the writing of the *Nicomachean Ethics*, see Jonathan Barnes, "Introduction," in *The Ethics of Aristotle* (Harmondsworth: Penguin Books, 1976) 9–43. For discussions of the way in which concrete debates and insights gave rise to principles in the tradition of casuistry, see Albert Jonsen and Stephen Toulmin, *The Abuse of Casuistry* (Berkeley: University of California, 1988) and James Keenan and Thomas Shannon, eds., *The Context of Casuistry* (Washington, D.C.: Georgetown University Press, 1995). For an account of current work in casuistry where this same movement can be observed, see James Keenan, "The Return of Casuistry," *Theological Studies* 57 (1996): 123–39.

movement from concrete insights into particular experiences, through successively more comprehensive insights and principles, towards concepts and principles that link together more and more diverse fields of experience.[57] In ethics, as in other fields of knowledge, we grow in understanding by moving from the particular to the general, from concrete insights to more fundamental principles.[58]

If moral knowing begins with insight into concrete experience and if moral foundations are not the first principles of logical systems, then how are we to think about moral "foundations"? Surely there is something that rings true about the textbook presentations. The philosophers and theologians were not misguided in their quest for coherence. Their theories have provided countless generations with extraordinary moral guidance. This guidance has taken the form of moral insights that can be applied by people to the numerous situations in daily living. If this guidance is not the guidance of logical first principles, then what is it? What sorts of things are moral foundations? And how do we reconcile an understanding of foundations with the diversity of moral theories?

This chapter explores some preliminary answers to these questions. The fact is, we know that such things as murder and rape are morally wrong. This is not simply a matter of individual opinion. Nor is it merely an arbitrary contract that we have made with each other. Our moral judgements and our societal laws involve real knowledge and our moral knowledge rests on foundations of some sort. In the following pages we will begin exploring some aspects of these foundations.

The strategy will be to proceed in five steps. The first involves a general discussion of foundations. What do we mean by foundations? How are foundations related to logical principles and theories? The second explores an interesting twofold thrust to moral action which has important implications for moral foundations. The third step examines how this twofold thrust works itself out in relations with other people and in wider social structures. The fourth step explores a

---

[57] John Noonan's accounts of the history of moral understanding on the topics of contraception and usury illustrate this movement. See his *Contraception* and *The Scholastic Analysis of Usury*.

[58] Lonergan discusses the movement from concrete insights through successively higher and more comprehensive viewpoints in *Insight*, Chapter 1.3.

novel way of understanding the term "freedom" and draws out some important links between foundations, pluralism, and ethical diversity. The fifth step describes some preliminary insights into a range of fundamental moral obligations that can be carried into various realms of life to direct our moral inquiry.

## Moral Foundations and Moral Persons

In order to get some notion of what we are looking for when we ask about moral foundations, let us begin with an illustration.

Early in civilization and, for each of us, early in our personal lives, we come to discover that there is something morally wrong with hurting other people. We also soon learn that there is something inadequate about this rule. In attempting to apply this rule, we discover an important moral difference between deliberate harm and accidents. Furthermore, when charged with protecting children, we discover that inflicting harm for personal gain is morally quite different from inflicting harm to defend the defenceless. Our understanding advances even further when we confront the moral significance of medical interventions which inflict harm to cure disease or repair injury. Soon, we start asking about the relations among all of these insights. What is foundational in all of this?

Each step along this path involves an insight into moral life. Clearly, such insights differ from insights in mathematics or physics. They engage our feelings in dramatic proportions, they spur us on to action, they subtly reshape our relations with others. Nonetheless, they are still insights: they are the fruits of inquiry and come only after considerable effort to make sense of our experiences. As we saw in the first chapter, there is a difference between fact-related insights and act-related insights, and both are subject to reflective scrutiny and judgement. We want to know if our insights are correct, if they are sound, if they are reliable guides for action. When we do this, we start asking about the coherence among clusters of insights and about the higher order insights which we will teach to younger generations. Finally, all of these operations yield questions and challenges for action. Moral knowledge is one thing; moral action is another. When we act on our knowledge, we verify and correct our knowledge, and we form ourselves as moral persons.

We might systematize the results of this process into a logically coherent theory, but the foundation of the process is not the logic of the system, it is the people performing the operations of insight, judgement, and decision at each step along the way.[59] Each of the insights involves a differentiation, a grasp of a morally significant difference, and we must know this differentiation not simply as an abstract formula but as a concrete reality for it to be moral knowledge. This can be done only by persons: each of us must perform the operations to attain the knowledge. Each differentiation results in a refinement of moral insights so that they apply more accurately to actual experiences. This differentiation must be understood, recognized for what it is, and affirmed in reflective judgement for it to be put into action in decision. This too can be done only by persons.

For any of us truly to learn this body of moral knowledge, we must get the insights ourselves. We must encounter the experiences and challenges which give rise to the questions, we must puzzle over the issues, we must hit on the insights which differentiate the general notions into more and more precise moral knowledge, and we must affirm them and appropriate them for our own living. The foundations of moral insights and judgements are persons. They are the persons engaged in the operations of moral knowing and doing in the various fields of life. Moral foundations are the states of capacities, skills, and virtues of persons required for authentic knowing and acting in these diverse fields.

Electricians, teachers, airline pilots, nurses, parents, and automobile mechanics all perform hosts of operations of insight, judgement, and decision throughout their working lives. In each case, the foundations for these operations lie only indirectly or remotely in the theories, books, and codes of their profession. As any master or mentor will insist, the competence is not in remembering the formulations, it is in the wisdom that comes from practice. It is in knowing how to bring the various tools of the profession, in their myriad combinations, to bear upon the diverse situations encountered in professional life. Furthermore, when this wisdom and experience are harnessed to advance knowledge in the profession, it is this same personal foundation that grounds the authenticity and worth of the new discoveries. The foundation of knowledge is persons. This is the case with professional knowledge; it is even more the case with moral knowledge.

---

[59] For a more developed account of foundations as converted persons, see Lonergan, *Method*, Chapter 11.

What remains true is that coherent moral theories can yield principles and methods that significantly enhance moral learning and performance in concrete life. When this is the case, however, the theories are not functioning logically, they are functioning *heuristically*. This means that the theories do not logically entail applications to concrete contexts; rather, they point persons in the direction where discoveries lie, leading them down paths of inquiry and investigation. The theories suggest the questions to ask and the data to gather, they point out potential problems and pitfalls, and they persuade by illustrating the collective merits of wide-scale implementation.[60] At each step along the way, the theories and principles do not supplant the personal operations of insight, judgement, and decision, but guide persons in the directions where past experience has found the most fruitful achievements to lie. For the results to be truly knowledge and authentically moral, the operations still have to be performed by persons. This is the case both in moral learning and in daily life.

## The Twofold Thrust of Moral Action

Moral foundations, then, are the characteristics and features of moral persons which are implicated in any concrete task of authentic moral knowing and doing. This is clearly the case when extreme situations call for obvious dedication, leadership, courage, or self-sacrifice: this is the stuff of epic films and legends. This is also the case in more mundane affairs. Parents are often called upon to make sacrifices for their children that test the limits of their moral capacities. In our business and professional lives, we frequently find ourselves struggling to decide between the easy road of mediocrity and the difficult road of integrity. In all of these cases, what is being tested is our moral foundations, who we are and what we have become as moral persons.

This foundational relationship between persons and actions is acutely obvious when we are challenged to live up to the requirements

---

[60] I am using the term "heuristic" in the same way that Lonergan scholars refer to the movement "from above downward." Knowing can proceed "upward," from experience to insight, through judgement, to decision. But it can also move "downward," from decisions and conversions, through judgements, to new insights and new openness to experience. For a fuller account of this two-way movement see *Method*, Chapter 5.5, particularly p. 142. Lonergan discusses this two-way movement in relation to the functional specialties in theology.

of known values. It is still more important when the challenge is the knowing itself. To arrive at reliable moral knowledge requires foundationally competent moral persons. This does not mean omnicompetence, it may not often mean moral heroism, but it does mean that authentic moral knowing will always require some state of personal moral achievement.[61] Thus the prevailing ranges of virtue of citizens will shape the relative quality of moral knowledge in society at any given time. This certainly has implications for the scholars, jurists, artists, and journalists whose job is to wrestle with the great moral issues of our age. The implications are even more significant for all of us who are charged with knowing the difference between lies and truth, cheating and fair-dealing, oppression and solidarity in the day-to-day events of life.

What is odd about this relationship between knowledge and persons is that, to a certain extent, the reverse is also true: if our knowing and doing are largely a function of our character, our knowing and doing can also have the effect of forming or transforming our character. Anyone who has followed a course of instruction in art, carpentry, or cooking knows that our range of capacities and skills at any point has a certain flexibility to it. As we move through the trial-and-error process of bringing extant skills to bear on new tasks, in new ways, and in new combinations, we move from clumsy performance towards smooth, automatic, and proficient mastery. Mastery or competence in a field consists in the attainment of the relevant skills and virtues in that field, but at any moment, our inventory of virtues and skills can be turned to new tasks and we can take some control over the development of foundations in new fields.

If this insight is obviously true in technical or artistic fields, it is far more profoundly true in moral knowing and living. This highlights the importance of structured programs of moral skill and character development for children and adolescents. This insight also brings to light a complex and hidden dimension of adult moral living: just as the musician continually reinforces and develops her skills in specific

---

61  This relation between moral knowing and moral achievement is the concern of "virtue ethics." See William Spohn, "The Return of Virtue Ethics," *Theological Studies* 53 (1992): 60–74; James Keenan, "Proposing Cardinal Virtues," *Theological Studies* 56 (1995): 709–729. See also Timothy O'Connell, *Principles for a Catholic Morality*, Chapter 6, for a discussion of the relation between moral actions and the character of moral persons.

directions through normal performance, so, too, our daily operations of moral meaning continually and subtly form our capacities, skills, and virtues in the same direction. While we focus our explicit attention forever on the issue at hand, the secondary and, in the long run, more significant upshot of our everyday decision-making is the shaping of our feelings, inclinations, and capacities for future moral knowing.

*Moral action always has a double thrust. The first and more obvious thrust concerns the issue at hand. The second and more profound thrust concerns the shaping of our moral character.* This second is the more profound thrust because today's character is foundational for tomorrow's deliberations. Our character tends to specify the general limits or parameters for the hosts of moral decisions we will be called upon to make tomorrow and the next day. Our normal inclination is to focus on the import of this decision for today's immediate context, but the significant thrust of this decision is its impact on our character and, thus, on our foundational capacities for tomorrow.

Moral action is self-constituting: it tends to reinforce the state of feelings, capacities, skills, and anticipations expressed by the actions themselves. When action harnesses the flexibility of our ranges of operations and skills to turn old skills to new tasks or to reinforce skill development in a new direction, this self-constituting thrust can lead decisively to growth. The effect will be a subtle shift in our feelings, capacities, and inclinations for subsequent knowledge and action. When we deliberately take up the task of shaping who we are becoming, our character becomes less a matter of social environment and more a matter of our own making. Still, transforming character takes a great deal of time; in the interim, we are stuck with the persons we have become through yesterday's decisions.

## Social Structure and Moral Foundations

This portrait of moral action as self-constituting might well ring true to aspects of our experience. It might just as well evoke a response of suspicion or criticism, however, a feeling that there is something wrong, something missing. Does this not portray a false image of ourselves as isolated individuals, and forget the massive discovery of this century, that humans are socially constituted? Are we not, at least in large measure, products of our historical and cultural environments? Have we not found that our conscious, deliberate living is only a small part of a much larger array of social forces operating to shape our characters and moral capacities?

To all of these questions, we must answer a qualified "Yes." Yet rather than negating the insights into the self-constituting structure of moral action, this discovery of the sociality of moral persons introduces a complexity to the process which can only be explained by recognizing morality's self-constituting thrust. This is because social forces are not mechanical or chemical or biological forces. They are structures and forces operating on the level of *meaning*. They work *through* our own operations of understanding, judgement, and decision, *not around* them.

Social structures exert a pressure on our personal moral knowing and acting to shift the direction of our performance and thus our capacities for future performance.[62] They do not supplant our knowing and acting; in fact, social forces draw upon and use the self-constituting thrust of moral action. Social forces work through our own operations of moral meaning to form our acting, which in turn forms our character and thus our capacities for future action. What is distinctive about social forces is the way in which other people's operations of knowing and acting come into the orbit of our own conscious life to shift the orientation of our own knowing and doing and to shape our sense of identity, our image of ourselves as persons. Because we are creatures of meaning, our capacities for action are formed in large measure by the ideas we have about ourselves, and it is these ideas that are most powerfully communicated in social interaction.

In interacting with others, we encounter a curious and powerful force which can go to the root of our sense of who we are and what we are about. This is the force of role-taking. In conversations with others, we get ideas, we initiate gestures, we tell them what we think and what we feel, and we portray hosts of other messages to them through our body language and our tone of voice. Yet this one-way speech is only the beginning of a complex interaction. These gestures set in

---

62 For a more developed discussion of the relation between social structures and moral knowing and acting, see Melchin, *History, Ethics, and Emergent Probability*, Chapters 6 and 7. For other discussions which draw on the work of Lonergan to discuss self-society relations in social ethics, see Chapter 1 of Matthew Lamb, *Solidarity with Victims* (New York: Crossroad, 1982) and John Raymaker, "The Theory-Praxis of Social Ethics: The Complementarity Between Hermeneutical and Dialectical Foundations," in M. Lamb, ed., *Creativity and Method*, 339–52.

motion a scheme of events that none of us plans, but that begins to unfold spontaneously the minute they respond to us.[63]

On occasion, we find that others respond to us precisely as we expect. Usually, however, we encounter differences. Their response may follow on our gesture, it may interpret our meaning, it may pick up a thread of what we intended, yet often it reveals a difference from what we intended or expected. The range of possible differences can be extremely large, but it is our response to these differences that is the key to understanding how social interaction shapes us. To one degree or another, our response is to wonder about their response, to try to imagine what they meant, to put ourselves in their shoes, to imagine ourselves as them listening to us, to take the role of the other and imagine them interpreting and responding to our gesture. This is role-taking.

Our role-taking is seldom fully accurate. Just as other persons often miss something of our meaning, so, too, we often miss something of their response. Still, in one way or another, we usually manage to glean some impression of ourselves as seen through their eyes. In trying to reconcile their response with what we meant, we begin to imagine how they understood what we said, what they thought we meant, the difference between what they thought we meant and what we actually meant. Most significantly, we begin to "see" how they "see" us as persons. Like all operations of meaning, this can happen in a split second or it can take long efforts of puzzling and probing. Still, as with all skills, the time intervals or the apparent unity must not delude us into misunderstanding the composite structure of the scheme. The spontaneous tendency to project ourselves into the position of others, to imagine their sense of our identity as it is manifested in their response to us, is one of the most complex and important features of human behaviour.

After a time of living in close proximity to significant others, the portrait of ourselves that emerges from this role-taking comes to assume a distinctive form. Our encounter with their image of us happens so frequently that we gradually take on this image virtually

---

[63] This analysis draws upon the works of Gibson Winter and George H. Mead and is developed in Melchin, *History, Ethics, and Emergent Probability,* 177–189. See also Melchin, "Moral Knowledge," 500–5.

wholesale as our own identity. Our self-image becomes a socialized identity. This is profoundly true in childhood when a parent's response to a child forges the pillars of her self-image and her character. It remains conspicuously true through adult life as well, even as we struggle to change or reshape this socialized image of ourselves. In fact, this effort would not be such a struggle were the effects of role-taking not so massive and enduring.

In our efforts to become our own persons, we not only take on our parents' particular ideas about ourselves, we also appropriate generalized notions of identity, personhood, and self-worth that are implicitly communicated and reinforced through the social routines of our culture. Images of gender, race, class, and profession are constantly being communicated by us and to us in the discourse schemes of daily life. Our inclination to role-taking invariably leads us to "become" our self-identity in accordance with these socialized images.

We are not merely passive receivers in this process; we are also active agents. Yet we are never the only agents. In role-taking, others make a major contribution to the constitution of our identity and relations, but a contribution which need not overrule our own input. On the other hand, while our capacity to author our own identity is always present, this capacity is never unlimited. The tendency, particularly in the early stages of childhood and adolescence, will be for others to make the larger contribution to who we are. This is not always a bad thing: it makes possible the awesome acceleration in learning and development which takes place in parenting and mentoring. As we progress in maturity, however, we strive to become authors of more and more of ourselves.

The socialization of identity goes both ways. Just as we remain part actor and part receiver in the formation of our own character, so too we are part actor and part receiver in the formation of others' characters. Thus the identity-constituting thrust of moral action has a further import for moral foundations, an import that links my action with the constitution of your foundations, and vice versa. In an extremely subtle and important way, our moral actions help constitute the moral foundations of our partner citizens in community and society.[64]

How do these points relate to our earlier observations about moral action as self-constituting? (1) While moral action does have a self-constituting thrust, this thrust is lived out in a scheme of social interaction in which others participate in the constitution of my identity, and in which my efforts to take control of my own character are continuously worked out in dialogue with others. (2) This socialization of identity by others is not so massive as to preclude responsibility for my own moral character, but it does suggest that becoming my own person will be a difficult thing, unfolding slowly through adult life. (3) The socialization of identity works both ways: I help to shape the moral foundations of others. I must accept this responsibility and carry it out in my interactions with them.

While we often think of discourse as the exchange of information, as if information were an external commodity to be transferred physically, discourse in fact involves a complex interaction between the interior states of persons. Role-taking with others can be nurtured or it can be refused; it can give rise to shared meaning or it can be challenged in conflict; it can be the means for mutual learning and mentorship, or for duplicity and exploitation. What is significant for our purposes is that this socialization scheme transforms the self-constituting thrust of moral action into a mutual or reciprocal constituting among people in communities and societies. *Our moral action is not only action, it is not only self-constitution, it is also participation in the shaping of the socialized and socializing identities of all of us in culture.*

## Freedom and Moral Foundations

To this point, our discussion of moral foundations has followed a path that an ethical theorist might say was in the stream of "virtue ethics."[65]

---

[64] For a discussion of how this mutual identity or character formation goes on in Christian ecclesial communities, see Stanley Hauerwas, *A Community of Character* (Notre Dame: University of Notre Dame Press, 1981). See also Gula, *Reason Informed by Faith*, and Happel and Walter, *Conversion and Discipleship*.

[65] See MacIntyre, *After Virtue*; Keenan, "Proposing Cardinal Virtues"; and Spohn, "The Return of Virtue Ethics."

If she did not agree with virtue ethics, she might suggest to you that this is, after all, only one theory, that there are diverse theories in ethics, that this diversity is *the* central or foundational problem in ethics, and that an account of ethical foundations must provide a basis for recognizing this diversity and our freedom to adopt whichever theory we choose.[66]

This criticism is important because it draws attention to the central idea of "freedom." If asked what is foundational in ethics, probably most of us would get around to talking about freedom. This is not just because we value our political freedom; it is also because we cherish our personal ethical convictions and become extremely nervous the moment someone else tries to push their moral rules upon us. There is something personal and inviolable about ethics which demands that we recognize freedom of choice. The more we are confronted with significant differences on issues like abortion, euthanasia, war, gay and lesbian rights, government spending, or free markets, the more we appeal to the fundamental moral obligation to respect the freedom of others. How can we talk about moral foundations without talking about freedom?

When we speak of freedom, of the basic rights that protect freedom, or of the institutions ordained to enforce these rights, we are using language most of us would consider foundational. To understand the links between our commitment to freedom and the portrait of moral foundations sketched here, let us begin by exploring two different ways of thinking about freedom. The first of these is probably the most familiar. It is the negative idea of freedom, *freedom from domination.* Here the typical image is an animal in chains, a person in prison, a victim of torture or brainwashing. Freedom, in this view, means breaking the fetters of bondage and releasing the victim. This image implies something else as well, a hidden dimension. This something

---

66   This critique is often formulated from the perspective of "liberal" theories in ethics. For a brief discussion, see Melchin, "Pluralism, Conflict, and the Structure of the Public Good," 77–82. However, the concern for an ethical theory which recognizes plurality is by no means restricted to this theoretical school. For a range of other approaches which take up this concern for pluralism in ethics, see the essays in Marc Lalonde, ed., *The Promise of Critical Theology* (Waterloo: Wilfrid Laurier University Press, 1995); and Dennis McCann, "The Good To Be Pursued in Common," in Williams and Houck, eds., *The Common Good and U.S. Capitalism*, 158–78.

else arises the moment we ask, "Release them to do what?" Here, of course, the difference between the animal and the person becomes significant. Whatever we might say about animals, the fact is that the answer for humans is, "To do what we choose!" It is in probing the implications of this answer that we are led to a second, not-so-familiar understanding of the term *freedom*.

(ii)     The second meaning of the term *freedom* is positive, not negative: it concerns the positive act of self-determination rather than the negative act of breaking or thwarting determination by others.[67] This self-determination need not imply complete control over self. Indeed, given our understanding of socialization, this notion of absolute self-determination is an illusion. What self-determination does mean is that through the operations of moral knowing and acting we can exercise a significant role in authoring our own actions. In our acts of raising and answering questions for moral knowledge and action, we exercise control over events. This control may not be complete, and it is never free from the input of others, but it adds a central determining ingredient to our actions, an ingredient that is uniquely our own. This is what freedom means in the distinctively moral sense: the capacity to perform the operations of moral knowing and doing.

This positive understanding of freedom as self-determination begins to connect with our account of moral foundations. Clearly, the central feature of this idea of freedom is our capacity to perform acts of moral meaning in which we size up situations, devise and evaluate courses of action, and begin to act on them. There is a difference, however, between speaking about the general capacity for self-determination, on the one hand, and, on the other, the operative ranges that define the limits of our actual abilities for self-determination at any particular moment. The truth is that these operative ranges are quite limited, and all too frequently they are far too limited. These limitations sometimes originate in our outer environment. Yet frequently this outer environment exerts its influence as we internalize it in our deliberations. Through much of life, it is our character, our extant virtues and skills, our moral foundations, that define the operative ranges of our freedom.

---

[67]  Lonergan's account of this positive understanding of freedom is developed in *Insight,* Chapter 18.2; and *Grace and Freedom*, ed. J. Patout Burns (London: Darton, Longman & Todd, 1971) 93–97.

This insight into the positive meaning of freedom gives rise to a distinction between essential freedom and effective freedom. *Essential freedom* refers to the capacity to exercise a determinate control over our own actions through the operations of moral meaning. *Effective freedom*, on the other hand, refers to the fact that the operative ranges of this capacity are restricted.[68] These restrictions, in the moral sense, are a function of the range of abilities, skills, virtues, feelings, and inclinations that we have become.

All of this, of course, brings us back to the issue of moral foundations. Our moral foundations are the persons we have become, and they define our actual ranges of effective freedom. This remains so even when we recognize the great role of socialization in the formation of personhood. Social forces are significant precisely because they are internalized and taken on as elements of our character. Our character is foundational for our effective freedom, but the social world exercises its influence over our effective freedom by shaping our character. It is precisely because of this foundational link between character and effective moral freedom that socialization plays such a formidable role in moral life.

When we begin examining the social and political context for transforming and expanding our ranges of effective freedom, this positive notion of freedom starts to connect more directly with our popular notions of freedom of choice. To develop morally, we must become "bigger" persons. This can be nurtured through social institutions, experienced mentors can guide this process, the support of others can accelerate its pace, and all of this can dramatically enrich the quality of achievement. Yet none of these can take our place for co-ordinating and directing our personal becoming. In this arduous process of adult growth, our own deliberations and decisions more and more form our moral character. This can never be done by another person. The responsibility for self flourishes best within the liberty provided by democracies.[69] Even when moral learning involves

---

[68] On the distinction between "essential" and "effective" freedom, see *Insight*, Chapter 18.3, and *Understanding and Being*, vol. 5 of *The Collected Works of Bernard Lonergan*, eds. E. A. Morelli, et al. (Toronto: University of Toronto Press, 1990) 226–34.

[69] Lonergan discusses this relation between democratic liberty and responsibility in the context of the reversal of bias and decline. See *Insight*, Chapter 8.4. For discussions on the way in which contemporary theories of the "common good" in

treading paths that are well worn, the process must always be one's own. This can involve discussion, argument, efforts to persuade, and, at times, even sanctions, but it can never be forced or pre-empted by another.

When the task involves pushing forward the frontiers of moral knowledge, the requirements of democratic liberty are even more acute. Wrestling with the great moral issues of an age is never a straight-line, smooth development: it invariably requires the hit-and-miss, trial-and-error efforts of experiment and innovation. For a few to succeed in discerning the lines of progress requires wide-ranging efforts proceeding along diverse paths of inquiry. Many of these will be mistaken; still, in ethics as in other fields of inquiry, the analysis of the failures yields clues to where success might lie.

This analysis demands that we recognize the difference between success and failure in moral action, between good and bad, right and wrong. Liberty does not mean obscuring or refusing this difference: it means respecting the freedom of inquiry, the process of moral development, and the people whose diverse views are integral to the task of striving towards common understanding on right and wrong. To affirm plurality and liberty in ethics is in no way incompatible with affirming the goal of common understanding of, and judgement on, good and bad, right and wrong. It simply requires understanding that the efforts towards this goal move forward through the self- and mutually-constituting decisions of persons, both in our personal lives and in our collective social living. Ethical pluralism means respecting the liberty and diversity that is essential for the collective discovery and appropriation of moral truth.[70]

---

the Catholic tradition are integrating the commitment to liberty and democracy, see the essays in Williams and Houck, eds., *The Common Good and U.S. Capitalism*, particularly Ralph McInerny, "The Primacy of the Common Good," 70–83, and Charles Curran, "The Common Good and Official Catholic Social Teaching,"111–29.

[70] Charles Davis presents a notion of pluralism which sees liberty and the respect for plurality as a requirement for the public pursuit of knowledge and value. See *Theology and Political Society* (Cambridge: Cambridge University Press, 1980) 168–69.

## Moral Foundations and Fundamental Moral Obligations

The previous chapter provided a range of insights into the social character of moral knowledge. In this last section, we begin exploring ways in which this understanding of foundations shapes our moral understanding and decision-making, and in particular, our fundamental moral obligations.[71] Finally, in an effort to link the discussion of these two sections, we will observe the role that the three levels of moral meaning play in fundamental moral knowledge.

Before doing this, however, we must consider briefly the difference between general or fundamental moral obligations, and specific moral obligations. If we are lost in a strange city and we are trying to make our way back to our hotel, the first thing we need to do is to get our bearings. Where is north? Where are the central landmarks? What is the overall layout of the relevant regions or districts of the city? Where are we in relation to all of these? Getting our bearings does not give us any detail about the houses or businesses on the streets, the ethnic makeup of the citizens, the relations among the people in the apartments, their occupations, their incomes, their artistic tastes, or their religious convictions. It does not tell us everything about the city; it does not even tell us everything about any one thing in the city. Yet it does tell us something, and this something is extremely important for us. In fact, it is absolutely essential. When we have established our bearings, they tell us what we need to know to set our journey in motion and to keep us on track.

Fundamental moral obligations are like getting our bearings. They provide us with a general map of the moral landscape, they provide us with tools for situating ourselves in relation to the most important moral landmarks, and they point out to us the directions of moral progress and decline.[72] As with the map and the city, they do not provide us with the concrete details of our journey, nor do they say much about the hosts of challenges that we will encounter along the

---

[71] One of the ways in which Catholic ethicists have discussed the notion of fundamental moral obligations has been in terms of the "fundamental stance" and "fundamental option." For a discussion of these notions, see Gula, *Reason Informed by Faith*, 78–81.

[72] For a similar presentation of "norms as authentic orientation," see Josef Fuchs, "The Absoluteness of Moral Terms," in *Readings, No. 1: Moral Norms and Catholic Tradition*, 127–32.

way or how to respond to these challenges, but they do provide the first essential tools for our journey, the layout of the landscape and the direction towards our goal.

To understand this landscape and the bearing provided by fundamental moral obligation we must identify a series of components and discover how the components work together. The *first* component comes from the first insight into moral foundations: if moral knowing and doing are founded on the persons we have become, and if moral action has the twofold thrust of constituting moral action and constituting moral persons, then *our fundamental obligation is to take responsibility for developing ourselves as moral persons through our moral action*. This may seem like a circular argument, but it appears circular only when we overlook the flexibility in our ranges of skills and capacities at any point.

Old skills and virtues can be turned to new tasks, thus developing new skills and virtues. We do this all the time. Because our capacities, skills, and virtues draw the limit or horizon for our moral knowing and doing, our fundamental obligation is to take responsibility for our capacities, skills, and virtues, and to push back this horizon. We must attend to the hidden side of moral action, that is, its self-constituting thrust, bring it into the foreground of our lives, and make it a chief concern in our decision-making. We want to act consistently in ways that push forward moral growth, especially throughout adult life.

The *second* component of fundamental moral obligation comes from the insight into the social structure of moral foundations. If moral action not only constitutes us as moral persons but helps reinforce and transform the general patterns of moral identity in culture, then *our fundamental moral obligation is to participate in reinforcing and developing virtuous patterns of social identity*. Here we recall our solidarity with others in the cooperative schemes of social living. Whatever we might have been led to think, we never "go it alone"; we are always in it with others. This second component of fundamental moral obligation is simply taking responsibility for this fact. It is our participation together in making one another's character, the foundations for moral knowledge and action, that is fundamental.

This second component has a direct bearing upon our insights into the social structure of moral knowledge, discussed earlier in Chapter 2. Concrete moral knowledge arises from the understanding of social structures and the way they impose obligations on participants. This implies that social structures will function only to the extent that citizens have developed the habits and virtues necessary for living up to these obligations. This second component of fundamental moral obligation speaks to our role in this wide-ranging development of public virtue. As fundamental, this obligation does not tell us anything specific about the content of these virtues, but it does require that we make their discovery and their proliferation our sustained personal concern.

Finally, the *third* component of fundamental moral obligation comes  from the previous chapter's insight into the three levels of moral meaning. The three levels of meaning are ranked hierarchically because in each case the higher level of meaning is more comprehensive. Each higher level can resolve problems and contradictions that seem unresolvable on the lower level. It is this hierarchical relation that provides the normative direction to the terms *virtue* and *development*. *Virtue* (as opposed to vice) and *development* (as opposed to decline) refer to the general direction of movement from self-interest, through social order, to the wider horizons of historical ordering and flourishing. *Our third fundamental moral obligation is to promote this development through the three levels of moral meaning, to remove obstacles that block this development, and to reverse forces that counter or undermine its thrust.*

Notice that what is normative here is not a fixed reference point or goal to this direction. Historical progress does not advance to a concrete content, event, or episode. Unlike the notion of "north" on a map, which might be identified with the magnetic north or the north star, what is normative here is a relation expressed between two moments in time. A better image might be the slope of a line or an incline. Progress or flourishing, in terms of the world we know, is not good because of the intrinsic "goodness" of a specific goal towards which things move or ought to move.[73] Instead, moral "goodness" or "rightness" expresses a relation between two historical moments.

---

[73] There is a distinction between progress in the world we know and the ultimate goal of the universe. In an absolute or ultimate sense, the goal of all things is God. However, within the range of human knowledge of history and society, progress is not defined by a concrete goal, but by a direction of change which is discernible and knowable as such.

Progress is the concrete form of this movement. We observe instances of progress all the time in our daily living: when we fall in love, when we are promoted in our jobs, when we are treated fairly, and when we encounter the generosity of others. We come to understand progress in a more general sense by understanding the relations among all these concrete instances of progress. The same holds true, of course, for our experience of decline.

The general features of moral progress are seen most clearly in the movement through the three levels of moral meaning, from self-interest, through social order, to historical flourishing. The structure of moral obligation changes when self-interest gives way to social responsibility. This growth or development from one level to the next is itself obligatory; indeed, it is more fundamental than the particular obligations we have on either of the two levels. This holds true when we shift to the higher level of historical responsibility. Not only are the obligations of each higher level more significant than those of the lower, but we are especially obliged to make this transition from lower to higher. This is what we mean by *self-transcendence*. We have the fundamental moral obligation to grow up and to continue growing up through all of our adult lives.

The three components of fundamental moral obligation are linked in a way that, at first glance, seems odd or contradictory. We often imagine the relationship between persons and society as a continuum, with persons at one end, society at the other, and the relationship in between. The image leads us to think that as action becomes more personal, it becomes less social, and vice versa. This is quite mistaken. Once we understand the self-and-socially-constituting structure to moral action, and once we understand the self-transcending dynamism expressed by the movement through the levels of moral meaning, we realize that growth towards moral maturity involves our becoming more self-determining, more socially responsible, *and* more meaningfully socially connected. Our fundamental moral obligations are to take responsibility for our self-constitution, to take responsibility for the constitution of social identity, and to appropriate self-transcendence as the norm for discerning what this responsibility entails. As we advance in our capacities to live out our fundamental moral obligations, we advance both personally and socially.

## Summary and Prospect

This brief discussion of the three components of fundamental moral obligation brings to a close the first part of our explorations. We began a journey of self-discovery in Chapter 1. Our effort was to gain some insight into the general experience of moral responsibility and the structure of operations which unfold in our deliberations and actions. While these operations have a general structure, they also function within horizons of meaning which both illuminate and conceal elements of our moral experience.

In Chapter 2, we turned to an examination of the social character of moral knowledge. After a series of clarifications by contrast, we explored three distinct levels of meaning of moral language and drew upon the example of the purchase transaction to gain some insights into "social structures." The analysis focussed on the links between the structure of the scheme and the obligations imposed on participants in the scheme. Finally, we showed how the three levels of moral meaning give rise to radically different modes of participation in social schemes.

In the present chapter, the focus has been upon ourselves as subjects or actors in these operations. In particular, we have examined how we are constituted and subtly transformed as social persons through our performance of moral operations. Insights into this have given rise to a distinction between a positive and a negative understanding of freedom. Finally, we have formulated three components of fundamental moral obligation that arise from this understanding of moral foundations.

In the two chapters that follow, the analysis changes direction: we turn our attention to Christian faith. What difference does faith make in moral deliberation? Through Part Two, we will work within the framework presented in Part One. Questions and observations about responsibility, moral knowledge, moral persons, and moral foundations will presume the distinctive meanings of the terms developed there. While we follow this strategy in hope of providing insights into the way our faith bears upon moral life, it may also pay off in a range of insights into Christian faith itself.

Through this second part, what also remains consistent is the focus on self-discovery. As with the previous chapters, the goal is not to marshal compelling arguments from authoritative sources; rather, the effort remains one of gathering insights into moral experience that help address some of the challenges facing us in our social living. This attention to self-discovery extends to religious self-discovery. Even the reader who lays no claim to a religious tradition may find points of resonance with religious concerns and their import for moral life.

*PART TWO*

# MORAL RESPONSIBILITY
# AND CHRISTIAN FAITH

*Chapter 4*

# What Difference
# Does Christian Faith Make?

To this point we have said nothing of Christian faith. Indeed, the account given so far might suggest that faith in Jesus Christ is not central to ethics, but simply an add-on, pleasant for some, secondary for others, quite unnecessary for those who feel they have outgrown childhood beliefs. Is ethics merely rational humanism? Does faith simply add authority to moral rules authored by reason? What difference does Christian faith make?[74]

To answer these questions, we will follow a rather novel line of inquiry, one that discovers a challenge in the midst of our moral lives, something that calls for a religious response. This is the challenge of evil. Before we begin, however, I offer an illustration to provide some idea of where we will be going in this second part of the book.

Have you ever wondered about the motion of a baseball? If you hit a baseball deep into left field, the path of the ball is often a smooth, unified trajectory. Yet we know that there are a lot of different factors that go into determining its path. The pitcher's action starts things off and, of course, the batter's swing exerts a formidable force on the ball, but tiny variations in the spin of a curve ball or a slider can have a dramatic effect on the final path. The surface of the bat, the friction of the air, the force of the gravitational pull of the earth, a breeze from the west, the surface of the ball, the effect of the lacing on the ball, all of these factors play a role in determining the final path. The precise contribution of each of these components could conceivably be measured and calculated for each hit. Nevertheless, the actual trajectory

---

[74]  For an introduction to recent literature on the relationship between Christian faith and ethics, see C. Curran and R. McCormick, eds. *Readings, No. 2: The Distinctiveness of Christian Ethics*; C. Curran and R. McCormick, eds. *Readings, No. 7: Natural Law and Theology*; James Gustafson, *Protestant and Roman Catholic Ethics* (Chicago: University of Chicago Press, 1978); James Gustafson, *Can Ethics Be Christian?* (Chicago: University of Chicago Press, 1975).

is not a jerky, cut-and-paste affair. It is a smooth unity which, on first glance, conceals its composite structure.

Moral actions are also composites. And, like the path of the baseball, their component parts are not immediately discernible to the untrained eye. Our response to a cry for help on a beach may unfold in a single, smooth action, yet the individual operations of questioning and answering can be differentiated. The dramatic import of this composite character comes to light when one of the key components is missing. On the beach, everything else may be in place, but if we do not care about the drowning person, the final result differs dramatically.

Christian faith provides a specific component to the trajectory of moral action. This is our commitment to morality itself because of our faith in God. Faith affects our commitment to moral deliberation and action, our commitment to other persons, our commitment to our moral growth and that of others, and our commitment to society and history as the arena where this drama of adult growth is played out. All of this is possible and it makes sense, not because we are guaranteed that our own efforts will succeed, but because we remain confident that God's grace is ever active in history, carrying forward our good efforts, and reversing the debilitating effects of our failures.

To clarify this, let us carry the baseball analogy one step further. We have listed a lot of components that shape the actual path of the baseball. Still, we have left out the most important one, the batter's commitment to the game. If the batter decides to stop trying, if she stops training to better her skills, if she gives up on her teammates in the middle of the game, the trajectory of the ball changes significantly. Even more significant would be the impact on successive hits as, time after time, the batter stepped up to the plate with a dwindling commitment to the game or a dwindling hope that her actions could make a difference.

Christian faith is not a set of divinely authored rules or principles from which we derive moral obligations. It is an enduring commitment to the worth of moral understanding and acting which is rooted in a confidence in God. And, like the batter's commitment to the game, it provides the central component which marshalls and gives direction to all the others. This remains so when the task is not simply acting out a known good, but vigorously pursuing the knowing itself.

All of this, of course, seems plausible to the converted. But to those of us who are skeptical, there remain serious questions. Why does this commitment to moral endeavour need to appeal to religion? Many of us grew up with religious practices which we remember as unpleasant or oppressive. Much of it seemed irrational, even absurd. When such memories are coupled with media reports of the devastation wrought by religious fanatics, we can be tempted towards a rather dim view of the place of religious faith in ethical living. Is religion compatible with a commitment to rational morality?

Our answer to this question will be straightforward: our lived response to evil has already thrust us into the realm of religion. We all recognize the pervasive fact of evil in our lives. What we may not recognize is how we have adopted responses to evil that bear an uncanny resemblance to religious claims. "You've got to fight fire with fire!" "If you can't stand the heat, get out of the kitchen!" "Only the strong survive!" These are familiar maxims that make comprehensive judgements about evil and how to live with it. Historically, they are tattered remnants of more complex creeds that originally had their roots in religious traditions. And all of them, while not explicitly religious in their language, make claims about our ultimate expectations in the face of evil. This is the realm of religion. When we take stands like those expressed by the maxims, we have already entered into the religious domain.

This chapter explores some troubling facts about evil which contest the simplistic stance of these maxims. Following the account of moral understanding presented in the previous chapters, we will ask if there is a problem arising in the midst of moral experience that calls for a more nuanced, a more differentiated religious response. The search here is not for a distinct body of material brought in from outside ethics, but for a dimension of our moral life that provokes a religious response. We will look for places where our reason turns towards questions of ultimate meaning and value, and towards answers that are rich and comprehensive enough to sustain us in our moral living.

The first half of this chapter is devoted to discussing the challenge which arises from the confrontation with evil.[75] The second half of this chapter takes up the response of the Christian tradition. The discussion here becomes quite tradition-specific, and here, one might say, we begin bringing in knowledge from outside of philosophical ethics.

---

[75] The principal resource for this line of analysis is *Insight*, Chapter 7.

Nonetheless, if the Christian faith response draws upon its own distinctive resources, this response is linked integrally and rationally to the very character of the challenge itself, as will be shown. Christian faith is not an alien intruder into ethical living; rather, it works within ethical experience as a response to the most dangerous and troublesome challenge in this experience, the threat of evil.[76] Furthermore, the aim of faith is not to derail or short circuit moral understanding; it is to empower reason in the face of obstacles which threaten to render us morally impotent.[77]

## Christian Faith as a Response to Evil

A recurring theme, key to all of Christian doctrine, is the theme of Redemption in Christ.[78] To understand what this could mean requires asking, "Redemption from what?" The answer, of course, is "Redemption from sin and evil!" and the challenge to which Christian faith is a response is the challenge of evil. While this language of redemption and sin might evoke memories of our catechism or Sunday school lessons on angels and devils, the reality of evil is more complex and more intimately a part of our experience.

---

[76] In *Grace and Freedom*, Lonergan presents Aquinas' account of how God's grace can be understood to operate without limiting or overriding human freedom. In fact, grace can be understood as an expansion of and condition for freedom. For an excellent discussion of this point, see Patrick Byrne, "The Thomist Sources of Lonergan's Dynamic World-View," *The Thomist* 46 (1982): 108–145.

[77] One might ask whether the Christian faith response to evil is unique, or whether elements are shared with other religious traditions. This issue is dealt with in the dialogue among world religions, and a number of scholars have drawn on Lonergan's work to analyse aspects of this dialogue. See, e.g., James Price, "Typologies and the Cross-Cultural Analysis of Mysticism: A Critique," in *Religion and Culture*, eds. T. Fallon and P.B. Riley (Albany, N.Y.: SUNY Press, 1987) 181–190; "Symposium: Lonergan's 'Philosophy and the Religious Phenomenon'," *METHOD: Journal of Lonergan Studies* 12 (1994): 121–179.

[78] Needless to say, the terms "redemption" and "salvation" have acquired meanings and connotations that can be quite misleading. One of these has been the legalistic meaning which conceives Christ's death and resurrection as a transaction, "buying back" a lost or forfeited state of grace. This legalism is not the meaning intended here. At the risk of being misunderstood, I have retained the traditional terminology because the alternatives appear to pose even greater problems. For an introduction to recent theological discussions on salvation and redemption, see Roger Haight, "Jesus and Salvation: An Essay in Interpretation," *Theological Studies* 55 (1994): 225–51.

Evil challenges all our ideas of justice and order. It pushes us to the limits of our faith in ourselves, in our loved ones, and in all aspects of our social living. Ultimately, it requires that we take a stand on the very foundations of hope itself, and forces us to face squarely the implications of our basic convictions regarding human finitude and ultimate value. More than anything else, evil forces us into the realm of religious questions.

For many of us, evil seems to be a rather straightforward affair: it is simply the refusal to do what we all know to be good. People who choose evil are evil people. The task of good people is to pursue the good and to fight those who are not!

The problem, unfortunately, is that things are not so simple. Evil seems to have an evasive quality, eluding clear identification in concrete life. Even when we feel we have named it, we often come across good people allied with it, as in Nazi Germany. Evil seems to be able to do its work quite apart from our intentions. It even has the nasty habit of harnessing good intentions to its own ends and rallying good people to its defence. It seems to have an extraordinary staying power, a comprehensive breadth of operations. Sometimes it is clear that concessions to evil are merely the failure of nerve or, worse, the pursuit of wealth or power. At other times, however, the picture becomes more complex and sinister. The older we get, the more evil we seem to see in good people and the more good we can see in bad people. In the final analysis, any simple hypothesis just does not work. As citizens of the modern, scientific world, we know that we cannot return to a language of devils, demons, and evil spirits. Still, if we are serious about the experiences of human history, the problem of evil most surely challenges the stereotypical portrait of "good guys" and "bad guys," and simplistic moral truths. *Evil is ambiguous.*

This analysis of evil builds upon the insights into moral knowing and moral persons from the preceding chapters. To this point, the discussions have focussed on understanding the structure of moral responsibility when it is unfolding successfully. Now we begin to examine what happens when it does not. Our moral knowledge and action is not always competent or responsible. We perform our ethical tasks imperfectly, and these imperfections can give rise to systemic evils that can wreak awesome havoc in social life. The massive reality of evil does not negate any of the insights developed to this point; in fact, it makes the concern for moral knowledge and action all the more urgent. It does mean, however, that we will need to be on the lookout for structures of evil as well as structures of good if we are to understand human affairs properly. So we need to have some idea of what we mean by "structures of evil."[79]

### Horizons and Moral Incapacities

One of the building blocks in our analysis of moral knowing was the notion of horizons. To say that moral knowing goes on within horizons is to say that we can break through constricting horizons to broader, more comprehensive understandings of life. In fact, we become aware of horizons precisely because such breakthroughs can and do occur. When we attend to these breakthroughs, we begin asking if and when further breakthroughs can be expected to occur, what we can do to prepare for them, and what we can do to accelerate their occurrence in ourselves and in others. This is the road of growth and development, the road towards maturity in our moral understanding and judgement, described above.

The consciousness of horizons, however, is also the consciousness of limitations, and limitations are not reserved simply for those past horizons that have given way to present understandings: they are also a feature of our present and future understandings and of our present and future capacities to understand.

To say that we live within horizons is to say that there will be realms of experience in which our moral knowing will be imperfect, flawed, incompetent. Now, imperfections can be managed when we can identify their precise location and make allowances for them. This is impossible, however, when we do not know that they are there. This is the case when the imperfections are in our moral knowing itself. Even if we aspire to a subtle grasp of our moral limitations, such a grasp is usually achieved only late in life, if at all. Meanwhile we go through our lives with an awesome ignorance of our limits in moral understanding.[80]

---

[79] Authors whose approach to Christian ethics is rooted in a critique of social evil include Gutiérrez, *A Theology of Liberation*; Gregory Baum, *The Social Imperative* (New York: Paulist Press, 1979). See also the discussions of the significance of the work of Habermas for theology in Don S. Browning and Francis Schussler Fiorenza, eds., *Habermas, Modernity, and Public Theology* (New York: Crossroad, 1992).

[80] Lonergan develops this analysis of "bias" in *Insight*, Chapters 6 and 7; and *Topics in Education*, Chapters 2 and 3.

What is true of moral horizons holds equally true for our ranges of effective freedom. None of us has an unrestricted range of effective freedom. The accent in this account has been on the internal conditions for effective freedom, the states of skill and virtue that expand the ranges of our capacities for moral knowledge and action. This explanation, however, only highlights the fact that moral activity within any given range will soon reveal both the potentialities and the limitations of that range. If the concern of the previous chapter was the potentialities, the present concern is the limitations. Again, because moral freedom is an activity of meaning, limitations in capacity will mean limitations in our ability to know when and where we have encountered our limitations. Of course, the fact of limits does not imply that we never know anything;[81] it simply means that as we approach the boundaries of our moral capacities, we can expect to find ourselves acting with the illusion of moral competence, only to find out later just how wrong we were.

The upshot of all this is that the analysis of the structure of moral knowing reveals a basic incapacity or incompetence that is a permanent feature of moral living. It is a shifting incapacity whose frontiers change as we develop towards moral maturity, and whose devastating effects can be curbed as we advance in self-knowledge, but it is nonetheless a permanent feature whose impact can be expected to be felt perennially in all aspects of our living. If our ethical goal is self-mastery, the basic tool for this task is the very self which is always in need of mastery.

## Bias, Habits, and Vices

Just as the analysis of the structure of moral knowing reveals the nature of moral incapacity, so too the analysis of the self-constituting character of morality shows how bad actions can grow into biases or vices, where evil becomes an automatic or habitual recurrence. Moral action is self-constituting. When this is understood, we can dedicate ourselves to the discipline of virtue formation. Disciplined practice involves the repeated performance of morally upright action to

---

81 Efforts to generalize from the facts of bias and ideology to the impossibility of moral knowledge invariably develop their arguments on the basis of some claim to moral knowledge. Usually this includes some sort of claim about the obligatory character of the relation between knowing and doing.

cultivate capacities and skills for moral action in ever-new realms of experience. Yet such virtue formation requires some prior knowledge of the good that we seek to cultivate. When this knowledge is lacking, or when it is subject to the limitations of moral incompetence, then discipline can just as easily form extraordinary vices.

In fact, repeated performance can cultivate bad habits even when it is not guided by deliberation and discipline. We frequently fall into patterns of dishonesty or self-interest where the consideration of others in specific situations is not so much refused as it is overlooked. To acquire bad habits requires only that such patterns be repeated often enough that they become the typical form of our response to such situations. We all know how easily such habits are formed, and how difficult it can be to extricate ourselves from their grasp.

Just as our capacities for good can be systematized and enlarged through the repeated performance of virtuous actions, so too can our capacities for evil be systematized and enlarged through routines of neglect or malice.[82] Again, because morality is an activity of meaning, newly acquired capacities and habits have the effect of subtly reshaping and adapting all other elements in our horizons of meaning. Consequently, while newly acquired habits seem startling and strange, they soon become familiar parts of our daily moral landscape and begin functioning as the tools which we take into new tasks. As habit transforms once-difficult action into effortless routine, evils that originated as momentary malice or failure become systematized into recurrent injury or offence. As they pass into the pattern of our living, they are taken up as the tools for solving new problems or for developing new capacities and skills. So, too, they become justified and rationalized within an overall moral logic that becomes ever more skewed as it is forced to accommodate ever more evil.

Thus vicious habits can stamp their imprint on broadening ranges of our lives quite apart from our deliberate intentions. What must be stressed here is not simply that evil occurs, that it can be deliberately chosen, or that it can become habitual, but that its effects can reach far beyond our explicit intentions. Because our moral actions are constituted by meaning, and because the tools for forging moral meaning are themselves operations of meaning, distortions or corruptions in the tools will be imprinted upon all realms of life

---

[82] Lonergan uses the term "individual bias." See his *Insight*, Chapter 7.6.

where they perform their work. Because the tools of meaning operate in the background of consciousness where they remain as invisible as the lenses of our own eyes, this stamping and imprinting will continue accelerating with little assistance required from the foreground of conscious intention.

## Ideology, Oppression, and Sinful Social Structures

Moral incapacity, bias, and vice are all rooted in the very structure of the person's moral knowing and acting. To understand their operation does not require grasping anything beyond this internal structure. As became apparent in the earlier chapters, however, the capacities and habits of individual persons are not the last word on moral life. Quite beyond the goods that are the work of individual persons, there remain the social goods that emerge in the cooperative structures of social and historical living. These goods can arise and function quite beyond anyone's plans. Conversations, families, friendships, business transactions, cities, economies, nations, and civilizations all have structures of interrelations that often are neither foreseen nor intended. Just as these social structures can harness the inputs of vast numbers of people towards the achievement of goods that none could have envisaged on their own, so too can they become agents of evils that far surpass the malice of individual people.[83]

Domination and oppression can be deliberately initiated by powerful individuals who promote their own interests at the expense of others. They can also achieve a far more comprehensive scale of operation when structures of social cooperation emerge in support of these interests. Oppressive social structures do not need to be planned. Social structures are linked sets of acts of meaning; the links can emerge spontaneously to yield structures that achieve what none could achieve alone, and these achievements can work for evil as well as for good. When societies are made up of different groups, the benefits accruing to one group can have devastating effects on others.

---

[83] For an introduction to the literature discussing "social sin," see O'Keefe, *What Are They Saying about Social Sin?*; Gula, *Reason Informed by Faith*, 116–21; Judith A. Merkle, "Sin," in *The New Dictionary of Catholic Social Thought*, 883–88; Neil Vaney, "Evil, Social," in *The New Dictionary of Catholic Social Thought*, 366–69; Patrick Kerans, *Sinful Social Structures* (New York: Paulist Press, 1974); Kenneth Himes, "Social Sin and the Role of the Individual," *Annual of the Society of Christian Ethics* (1986): 183–218.

As long as the emergent structures are not acknowledged, analysed, and evaluated, their horrific impacts on marginalized groups can continue unchecked without anyone deliberately intending harm.

Oppression becomes most acute when powerful groups recognize the operation of such emergent structures, recognize the benefits accruing to them from the status quo, and exercise their power to keep them in place.[84] Notice, however, that this is a very different type of evil than that which is devised and initiated by individuals. When emergent structures are involved, the extent of influence is increased well beyond the range of any individual's intention. Furthermore, it is easy for parties implicated in the advantages to misconstrue the moral character of their own involvement in structural evil. When we are far from the experience of their horrifying effects on others, it is easy to delude ourselves into minimizing their import or rationalizing them as necessary or unavoidable. This is particularly appealing when the same social structures yield real benefits for our loved ones. Such forms of oppression are more intractable because they often achieve real goods for some participants, and this moral knowledge recruits the efforts of countless well-intentioned citizens to the task of defending the scheme against efforts to change it.

Thus structures of social meaning can become agents for a large range of social evils. As we are raised within these structures, we come to accept them as part of the "natural" background of social life. They become part of the ideology of everyday living: we absorb them into our habits of meaning, and our daily actions are subtly directed towards sustaining and defending them.

One could ask how we are to allocate blame in such instances, but this question threatens to force the moral analysis of social life into a framework foreign to the distinctive structure of social evil. This does not mean that there is no blame for social evil, but it does mean that there remains a surplus of evil beyond what can be ascribed to individuals.

---

[84] Lonergan develops his distinctive analysis of social sin in *Insight*, Chapters 7.7, 7.8, 18.3, and 20.1. Other authors who discuss this aspect of Lonergan's work include O'Keefe in Chapter 5 of *What Are They Saying about Social Sin?*; Lamb, *Solidarity with Victims*, Chapter 1; William Loewe, "Dialectics of Sin: Lonergan's *Insight* and the Critical Theory of Max Horkheimer," *Anglican Theological Review* 61 (1979): 224–45; and Melchin, "Military and Deterrence Strategy."

Here, of course, is where the issue starts to get religious. How can this be? How can a good God permit such a state of affairs? It cannot be God's fault! So it must be some person's fault! The sceptic or the unbeliever, on the other hand, accepts the facts but finds them to be further evidence against the existence of God. Still, the problem of the reasonableness of moral commitment remains. Given the magnitude and scope of evil, a fully good life seems impossible. If evil were simply a matter of individual choice, then we could blame things on evil people. But this does not seem to be the case.[85]

How are we to marshal our commitment to the good when we seem to be undermined in our efforts at every step along the way? To do good requires effort, commitment, dedication. How are we to muster this effort when we can expect to be thwarted by invisible and faceless forces of social evil on every front? Why bother to be moral? If we choose to continue the effort, in what can we hope?

## The Religious Problem of Hope and Despair and Its Significance for Moral Living

There is a conventional wisdom floating about that seems to make a virtue of despair. One group would say that, on the basis of the foregoing analysis, we should abandon lofty ideals and recognize that only evil can combat evil. Morality is a silly illusion; it is not the way the world really works: we must fight fire with fire! A second group would say that the force of ideology is so widespread that we can never know the difference between evil and good. We cannot know what is truly good and so we must settle with our personal views and stop foisting our moral opinions on others. A third group would renounce the entire task of moral dedication and invite us to live for ourselves, live for today. What are we to make of these responses?

The first thing we can observe is that all of these responses involve a contradiction. It is a contradiction between the content of the claim

---

[85] For a discussion of Lonergan's analysis of the improbability of morally good action, given the magnitude of evil, see *Grace and Freedom*, 41–42; Byrne, "The Thomist Sources," 110–12. Barry Whitney presents an overview of various efforts to reconcile God's power and goodness with the fact of evil in *What Are They Saying about God and Evil?* (New York: Paulist Press, 1989).

and the implicit thrust of the claim.[86] In each case, the implicit thrust of the claim is to champion the chosen course of action as the reasonable or moral thing to do. It is the only choice that makes sense. The evidence for it is compelling. To accept it is to accept the world as we know it. To refuse it is folly. The implicit thrust of each is that it is the *truly moral* thing to do. And in each case, the content of the claim refuses the possibility of such a moral claim.

In the first and third cases, the contradiction is between the implicit moral thrust of the claim and the invitation to ignore or contravene this normative thrust in our deliberation and action. In the name of morality we are urged to abandon morality! In the second case, the contradiction is between the implicit claim to moral knowledge and the explicit denial of the possibility of moral knowledge. In the name of morality we are urged to face up to the fact that we can't know what is truly moral! And in all three cases, the assumption is that moral renunciation or accommodation to self-gratification does not make things worse.

This assumption is false. Things will get worse! The proposed solutions can only exacerbate the problem, because moral meaning is self- and socially-constituting. What arises in each of these responses to evil is a greater problem than the evil that it confronts. It is the refusal or paralysis of the most basic exigence to responsibility that is the very ground of our capacity to resist evil. Because moral life is an affair of meaning, what we think about moral meaning will eventually shape our capacities for moral meaning and action. Because our capacities are socially and not just individually constituted, there can arise social structures to support this moral renunciation, thus becoming the normative public consciousness. Because normative consciousness establishes what is considered "natural" and "real," subsequent generations become incapable of imagining any alternative to the renunciation of responsibility. The proposed solutions surely involve a contradiction, but social structures do not await the resolution of contradictions to emerge and flourish.

The principal issue here is the issue of hope. Given the situation as described thus far, in what shall we hope? While this is a question that

---

[86] Lonergan discusses various aspects of the contradiction implicit in general bias, the longer cycle of decline, and moral renunciation. See his *Insight*, Chapters 7.8, 18.1.2, 18.3.4, 20.1, and 19.9, pp. 689–91 (1957 ed., pp. 666–68).

arises from our analysis of the structure of moral life, it is nonetheless a religious question. In the final analysis, it is a question about ultimate meaning and value. It is a question about the object or goal of the dynamism of responsibility that animates our own lives. It is a question whose answer will affect our ability to live out this dynamism. This thrust towards responsibility that animates every aspect of our living is a vector which points in a direction. What is this direction?

## What Difference Does Christian Faith Make?

Christian faith is not a set of ethical principles, nor is it a compelling logical syllogism that leads all rational persons to necessary conclusions. Rather, at its centre lies an event or an experience that occurs in life. Faith is the testimony of persons who have encountered the power of God who is forever at work in human history, breaking the bonds of evil and restoring hope when hope has been lost. Christian faith is the attitude of confident expectation that, in some mysterious way, God is at work both personally and socially and that we can experience this activity time and again through our lives. This faith restores our commitment to responsibility when evidence would incline us otherwise. The most critical effect of this faith is to halt the radical acceleration of evil that occurs when we give up on the possibility of the good.[87]

Moral meaning has a cumulative power. What we think about our moral capacities shapes the way we perform the operations of moral meaning. This performance moulds our habits, it sets ranges for the sorts of social arrangements that can emerge in life and, consequently, it sets the conditions for the emergence of social events that accumulate quite apart from our explicit deliberations. When we remain committed to the good, the effect of this commitment multiplies beyond our deliberate intentions. When we give up on the good, the effect of this despair also multiplies and accumulates. Christian faith halts the

---

87 This presentation draws upon *Insight*, Chapters 20.2, 20.3; *Topics in Education*, Chapter 3.1.3; *Method*, Chapters 4.3, 4.4. See also Lonergan, "The Redemption," in *Philosophical and Theological Papers 1958–1964*, vol. 6 of *The Collected Works of Bernard Lonergan*, eds. R. Croken, F. E. Crowe, and R. M. Doran (Toronto: University of Toronto Press, 1996) 3–28; Lonergan, "Healing and Creating in History," *A Third Collection*, ed. F. E. Crowe (New York: Paulist Press, 1985) 100–109; and Sebastian Moore, "For a Soteriology of the Existential Subject," in Lamb, ed., *Creativity and Method*, 229–48.

accelerating effects of despair and restores our commitment to the good, not by refusing the reality or the magnitude of evil, but by acknowledging that our limited power in the face of this evil is only part of the picture.[88]

The foundation of morality is the exigence or dynamism of responsibility whose analysis has been our concern throughout these chapters. While this exigence is foundational, it is neither necessary nor fully determining; rather, we experience this exigence as an urge or inclination that, frequently, is merely one inclination among others. It is up to us to choose this exigence or to reject it as the guiding force in our moral deliberations and actions. To make this choice, time and again, requires considerable energy and dedication. When our experience of evil brings us to the point of giving up on this arduous task, faith in Christ restores this commitment by revealing to us a divine power that is operative in history. When we choose the good, we do not work alone, but our efforts are complemented by the saving work of God whose power knows no bounds.[89]

The form of this encounter with the saving work of Christ is love. It is the experience of love that refuses to return evil for evil. It is the refusal to return hate when we are hated, the refusal to give up on ourselves and others when actions warrant condemnation, the refusal to seek retribution in kind when we have been victimized. Love does not give up on justice, but it distinguishes moral action from moral

---

[88] This analysis of God's redemptive response to evil does not imply that God's work of grace is an afterthought, only entering history to correct a defect in creation. Grace and redemption are present in the very act of creation itself. However, the most significant challenge for human moral action lies in coming to terms with human finitude and sinfulness. Consequently, Lonergan's approach to grace, particularly in Chapter 20 of *Insight*, focusses on our encounter with charity as a response to moral impotence. For a discussion of the creative and redemptive aspects of grace, see Lonergan, "Healing and Creating in History," in *A Third Collection*, 100–109.

[89] A considerable number of authors have explored the implications of Lonergan's work for a theology of grace and salvation. See, e.g., William Loewe, "Towards a Responsible Contemporary Soteriology," in Lamb, ed., *Creativity and Method*, 213–28; Stephen Happel, "Sacrament: Symbol of Conversion," in Lamb, ed., *Creativity and Method*, 275–90; Sebastian Moore, "Soteriology"; Louis Roy and W. W. Meissner, "Toward a Psychology of Grace," *Theological Studies* 57 (1996): 322–37. For an introduction to contemporary discussions on grace and salvation in theological literature, see Roger Haight, "Jesus and Salvation."

persons, and condemns evil action while refusing to give up on persons. The full requirements of this love are surely beyond human capacities, but Christian faith adamantly refuses to accept human capacity as the whole story. The full truth of human living is told in the mystery of salvation history, in which God's saving grace is revealed in its total and ever-present reality. This was the foundation of hope of the early Christians, and it is the foundation that repeatedly renews the commitment to responsibility of succeeding generations of Christians. It is the foundation of love that is possible because of God's love ever at work in us.[90]

Much more needs to be said here. How is this experience of love made known? How can we distinguish authentic religious convictions from inauthentic or destructive religious claims? How is such a belief in the supernatural compatible with a scientific world view? All these questions are important, but what we need at this point is an understanding of the structure of the moral problem of evil, its debilitating consequences for moral living, and the role of Christian faith in reversing the accumulating effects of evil.

Faith in Christ is not a special or secret knowledge, available only to the elect, which reveals special obligations beyond those that can be known by human reason. It is instead an encounter with a transcendent reality within the range of human experience that corrects a fundamental deformation in moral responsibility itself. Faith restores the very commitment to moral knowing and acting that is eroded or eclipsed when we are overwhelmed by the magnitude of evil in the world. It does so, not by turning away from the reality of evil, but by turning towards the memory and the testimony of men and women through the ages who have encountered God's saving power and made it their own in the midst of evil. Faith empowers moral reason to do its work and its vehicle is the testimony of encounter.

## The Ethics of the New Testament:
## The Early Christians' Encounter with the Risen Christ

For the Christian, the most dramatic and definitive testimony to the encounter with God's redemptive grace is the testimony of the early Christians in the New Testament. We can expect the healing power of grace in our lives because this power has been revealed to us as an

---

[90] See *Insight*, Chapter 20.3.

event which can and does occur in history. It was the experience of the early Christians, and their testimony to this experience has been left to us in the books of the New Testament. As we read and re-read the texts, as we pray them in our private lives, and as we proclaim and celebrate them in our public liturgies, we are introduced to the overall character of this divine power, and we are furnished with tools for discerning its occurrence time and again in everyday events.

As in all fields of human expertise, indeed, as in all fields of human experience, if we wish to understand we must nurture and develop the skills for discernment and judgement appropriate for that field. So it is with faith; faith is the encounter with God's healing response to sin, and in praying and celebrating the scriptures, we forge the tools for this faith discernment. What we find in the scriptures are the stories of those whose lives have been liberated from the power of evil. Their witness furnishes us with confidence to expect this power in our own lives, and familiarity with their stories helps and guides us to recognize this power when it meets us.

This testimony to the encounter with the risen Christ is the core of the ethics of the New Testament.[91] We might expect that the expression, "ethics of the New Testament," refers to a code of conduct or a book of rules. For the most part, however, these expectations would be mistaken. Through the ages, the efforts of scholars to compile such a code from the scriptural texts have led to little agreement. In fact, there seems to be a strong thematic bias against code-type or legalistic ethics, both in the Gospels and in the letters of Paul. What scripture scholars have found is that the New Testament contains a different type of ethical teaching, an ethic of the Kingdom of God, an ethic of grace.

Both the earthly ministry of Jesus and the life of the early Church focus not on what we must do to build a good society, but on what God is doing in the middle of our daily lives. Throughout the Gospel

---

[91] The following discussions draw upon E. Clinton Gardner, "New Testament Ethics," in *The Westminster Dictionary of Christian Ethics*, 421–24; J. L. Houlden, "Jesus, Ethical Teaching of," in *The Westminster Dictionary of Christian Ethics*, 316–20; Rudolf Schnackenburg, *The Moral Teaching of the New Testament*, trans. J. Holland-Smith and W. J. O'Hara (New York: Herder and Herder, 1965); Wayne Meeks, *The Origins of Christian Morality* (New Haven: Yale University Press, 1993); and Ben F. Meyer, *The Early Christians: Their World Mission and Self-Discovery* (Wilmington, Delaware: Michael Glazier, 1986) 159–71. I am indebted to Normand Bonneau for his insights here.

texts of the earthly preaching of Jesus, the consistent emphasis is upon the Kingdom of God. Jesus repeatedly calls his disciples to pay attention to God's presence, to God's work in their lives, and to God's dramatic call for repentance and participation in this work. God is not a distant creator who starts the world in motion and then sits back to watch us struggle to do what we should. Rather, Jesus proclaims a God who is active! Our principal obligation is to open ourselves to the power of this action and allow it to work in us. Jesus' language of the Kingdom of God is the principal symbol of this ever-present action.

If the focus of the Gospels is Jesus preaching the Kingdom of God, the focus of the Acts of the Apostles and the letters of Paul is the death and resurrection of Christ. God's act of raising Jesus from the dead is the definitive proof that God is at work inaugurating the Kingdom. Jesus' earthly life ends in tragedy and failure because of the power of structural sin. The symbol of the cross is the sign of this ever-present power of evil in the world. Even Jesus, the greatest leader they had ever seen, falls victim to the power of evil. Yet the crucifixion is not the end of the matter, for God raises Jesus from the dead! His resurrection is the final confirmation that the power of sin, with its legacy of tragedy and failure, can never be the whole story. The resurrection of Christ is evidence to the disciples that God is transforming the moral efforts of humans, extending our good efforts and reversing our failures.

This message, the central message of the New Testament, is the core of Christian ethics. Ours is an ethic of responsibility, but it is a distinctive form of responsibility, a responsibility which must recognize the debilitating power of sin and the transformative power of redemptive grace. Alongside the good that we do stands the ever-present reality of evil, deforming our aspirations, corrupting our projects, and undermining our achievements. This power of evil is not ours to vanquish once-and-for-all, but neither is it the last word in the drama of society and history: the final word is spoken by God. Our moral efforts, corrupted as they are by sin and evil, are also part of a larger drama in which God is mysteriously working to bring to reality the fullness of the Kingdom. The ultimate scope of this larger drama is not restricted to human history: it is beyond history. Yet it is still operative in history, doing its transformative work, and issuing its summons for our participation. For Christians, responsibility means taking the risk of entering into the mystery of this greater drama, through the decisions and actions of our everyday lives.

### Progress, Decline, and Redemption: Christian Responsibility in Society and History

The net result of all of this is a rather curious way of understanding our responsibility for the events of society and history. Normally we think of ourselves as responsible for social life. Furthermore, we think that responsibility means full responsibility. Either we are responsible or we are not. Either we take charge of our actions, or we hand ourselves over to the charge of another person or another power. The Christian insight into sin and grace, however, would suggest that responsibility is never *sole* responsibility. Our own moral action is never the only thing at work in shaping the course of events: the powers of sin and grace are also at work. Still, we must take charge of our actions. Paradoxically, taking charge means, in some way, handing ourselves over to the charge of another, to the work of God. In the end, this handing over is itself an empowerment; it is a renewal and enhancement of our own capacities for responsible action in social life.[92]

To understand the events of society and history, we must recognize that social life will seldom result from the action of single causes. Rather, we can expect that events will be the outcome of interactions among three sets of forces: progress, decline, and redemption.[93] Our understanding of these forces provides us with analytical tools for understanding events. For these tools to prove helpful in making sense of things, we must learn to discern how they interact in concrete situations and give

---

[92] Kenneth Himes presents a discussion of the relation between social sin and personal responsibility in "Social Sin and the Role of the Individual." For a discussion of responsibility as response to God, see Albert Jonsen, "Responsibility," in *The Westminster Dictionary of Christian Ethics*, 545–49. For a discussion of the relation between "moral impasse" and grace, see Constance Fitzgerald, "Impasse and Dark Night," in *Women's Spirituality*, ed. Joann Wolksi Conn (New York: Paulist Press, 1986) 287–311.

[93] Lonergan uses the term "differentials" to refer to what I have called the three "forces." See his *Topics in Education*, Chapter 3, and Michael Shute's *The Origins of Lonergan's Notion of the Dialectics of History* (Lanham, MD: University Press of America, 1993), particularly Chapter 2.

rise to results which often do not look at all like any of the forces individually.[94]

To speak of a Christian faith perspective on society and history is to say that we can expect to find progress, decline, and redemption at work in the normal course of human affairs. To be sure, we can expect our explanations of events to go forward on various levels of analytical complexity.[95] What is important for our purposes is the way that this perspective forms our ideas about our role in social events. If structures of sin and the power of grace are at work in social affairs, then we can expect to find serious problems in simplistic explanations that reduce events to our own capacities to promote moral progress. Furthermore, we can expect to find disastrous consequences if people respond according to such simplistic analyses.

For example, from this Christian faith perspective we must admit that sin and evil will never be eradicated from political life. As we watch the evening news or read the papers, we can expect that day-to-day events will be fraught with evil, failure, corruption, and ideology. We can expect that our leaders will fail us, even betray us, sometimes because they are corrupt, sometimes because of bias and ideology, sometimes because the problems are simply beyond them, and sometimes because of structures of evil in which we participate unwittingly. Sometimes they will fail us because *we* are mistaken in what we demand of them. To react to these events with outrage and blame is to forget structural evil. It is to suppose that events are determined solely by human moral capacities. Furthermore, it is to forget that, in some mysterious way, redemption is present and active even in the midst of the most tragic political events.

Similarly, we are regularly invited by the media to pronounce judgement on our criminal justice system. Daily stories of overcrowded courts, repeat offenders, acquittals on technicalities, and privileges accruing to the wealthy lead us to despair and rage over the deterioration in social living that must surely follow these things. Again, the implicit assumption here is that regular progress in our justice system is indeed achievable through our moral efforts, and that failure must be eradicated. If the course of events, however, is not one of moral

---

[94] See *Topics in Education*, 69–70.

[95] On differences in levels of complexity of the explanations, see *Topics in Education*, Chapter 3.2; see also Chapters 5, 6, and 7.

progress alone, but arises from the interaction of progress with the forces of sin and grace, then our evaluation of events takes a different turn. We are led to ask about the permanent, ineradicable presence of sin in such a system. In certain cases, the current state of affairs could be viewed as a work of heroism in the face of monstrous obstacles. Once again, as our analytic efforts turn to the search for traces of God's redemptive grace, we come to appreciate the significance of a system which is dedicated, not to retribution, not only to deterrence, but to the correction of the offender.

These are merely brief sketches of the direction that such analyses might take. Nonetheless, they do begin to reveal the traps and pitfalls that arise when we have simplistic, reductive perspectives on social life. Furthermore, they reveal the problems that can arise when we make simplistic analyses the foundation for corrective social action. Repeated efforts to explain political events as the conspiracy of elites erode social confidence in public institutions. An ever-growing fear of crime which arises from a widespread critique of the justice system erodes public trust among citizens. In both cases, the webs of public confidence and trust which are foundational to all aspects of community, economic, and political life, begin to give way.

A Christian faith perspective on social responsibility attacks this problem at its core, not with a denial of conspiracy or systemic corruption, nor with a naive confidence in the goodness of humanity, nor with a naive hope in an order secured through mortal combat or revolutionary upheaval. Instead, faith recognizes that God's trans-forming grace is already at work in these social events, undoing the effects of sin and correcting the labours of responsibility. When we work to restore justice, we do so with an attitude of humility, grati-tude, and joy: we expect that our efforts towards progress, while limited and corrupted by sin, will be transformed and complemented by grace. We can never give up on our responsibility for social life, either in complacency or in despair, but the form of our responsibility is forever tempered by the expectation of sin and grace. As we grow in moral and spiritual maturity, our tools for discerning the diverse patterns of interaction among progress, decline, and redemption be-come ever more differentiated, and ever more effective as guides for understanding and assessing the trajectory of our moral action.

Responsibility for the Christian is always co-responsibility; it involves cooperative action with other women and men. Most importantly, it is cooperation with God. We can never think of our moral action, either individually or collectively, as the final, definitive power at work in our families, our communities, or our social-political lives. We have an obligation to act ethically, but Christians must acknowledge the limits of our moral capacities, and open ourselves to the mysterious drama of God's grace active in our personal and social lives.

## Summary

This analysis has introduced the role of Christian faith in moral life by presenting faith as the encounter with God's redemptive grace, and grace as God's response to the problem of sin. Social living is the enterprise of people cooperating in structures of action that achieve results far beyond what individuals could achieve on their own. These structures implicate us in goods as well as evils. In our daily experience it is not difficult to accept the goods as a matter of course. It is something else, however, to accept the evils.

Structural evil is more than the intentional malice of individuals, it is more than the ideology which is supported by power and authority. It is a dynamic of decline: cooperative social structures sustain deformed notions of the good, they promote the interests of some at the expense of others, they harness the cooperation of well-meaning persons in service of their tasks, they accumulate by forming the habits of successive generations of citizens, and, eventually, they provide ample evidence to all that morality is an impossible or silly ideal. Sin is a power in social and political life that radically circumscribes and compromises the capacities of moral responsibility.

Christian faith is the encounter with God's reversal of the debilitating effects of sin and restoration of moral action. It is not merely a belief in responsibility which stands in the face of the forces of evil, it is not merely a conviction that good will someday overcome evil: it is a personal encounter with the power of grace that restores us as responsible agents of this good. It is also a recognition that this power is a mystery and a gift, revealed most fully in the death and resurrection of Christ.

The consequence of this is a Christian faith perspective on social responsibility. The events of social life are shaped by three sets of forces: progress, decline, and redemption. Efforts to reduce events simply to one or another of these forces result in simplistic and destructive analyses. The patterns of interactions among these forces are complex, and we must forge tools in order to discern properly past events and present responsibilities. In the next chapter, we introduce some of these tools and briefly discuss how they work in our moral deliberations.

*Chapter 5*

# Christian Faith and Moral Deliberation

Often things are not what they seem. If we were to take off a shoe, grab the laces, and whirl the shoe around our heads, we would find (if the laces were long enough) that we could make the shoe spin around our heads in a pattern something like a circle. Yet, if we were asked to explain this circular motion, we could not answer by appealing to a single circular force, for the motion was not caused by a single force. Instead, we would have to say that the circular motion resulted (roughly) from the interaction of three distinct forces: the force of our hand propelling the shoe outward, the force of the laces holding the shoe inward, and the force of gravity. Furthermore, we would have to admit that, for the most part, none of these forces were circular; they were linear. Who can imagine this? None of these forces individually looks anything like the final result of their interaction. Yet this is how it is.

If we knew enough about physics and mathematics, we could explain in theoretical detail how the three linear motions could result in a circular motion. If we did not know physics and mathematics, our explanation would have to remain on a simpler, common-sense level, and there would be a limit to what we could achieve in the explanation. Yet the facts of the situation remain.

Explaining the events of society and history from a Christian faith perspective is something like explaining the circular motion of the shoe. Our faith perspective provides us with three analytic tools for understanding human affairs: *progress, decline,* and *redemption.* Christians can expect that a study of events will reveal evidence of *moral progress.* It will reveal personal acts of responsibility as well as our participation in cooperative acts of responsibility which accumulate socially and yield fruits according to a structured dynamic of historical progress. We can also expect to find evidence of *sin and decline.* Again, the most potent form of this decline is not the evil that individuals intend, but the social structures of evil which proliferate according to the dynamics of vice, bias, ideology, oppression, impotence and despair. Finally, we can expect to see evidence of *redemption*. God's redemptive grace is mysteriously at work, ever-present, ever-active in the events of society and history, reversing the effects of sin and advancing the work of responsibility.

To this point, we have developed the components of this faith perspective and assembled them into a framework for understanding the events of our lives. In this chapter, we show how this perspective shapes moral deliberation. Our understanding of history dramatically affects the way we understand our obligations for shaping the course of social events. This is especially so if we think that other powers from within and beyond history exert an influence on our actions. To recognize our moral efforts towards progress as one component in a triad of interacting forces shaping history is to reconceive the character and direction of responsibility. This chapter begins to sketch some features of this new conception.

The aim of this sketch is not to capture the details of particular moral issues; rather, it is to illustrate what begins to happen to the direction and nature of our moral deliberation when we understand our efforts to be subject to the forces of sin and redemption. We begin with four themes which appear frequently in theological literature: God's justice; the dignity of persons; the common good; and the preferential option for the poor. Throughout the discussions we will see how each establishes a direction for our moral deliberations and how this direction is integrally linked to an understanding of the impact of sin and redemption on human responsibility.[96]

Finally, we will conclude with some methodological insights into the relation between general principles and specific moral contexts. The themes sketched here reveal a general direction to moral deliberation but they do not offer specific obligations that are immediately applicable to situations. What is the relation between general principles and specific contexts? We are often instructed to "deduce" concrete implications from general principles. Is this what goes on in moral deliberation, or is there a different relation between the direc-

---

[96] While a considerable literature has been devoted to each of the topics of this chapter, the discussions here will be brief and introductory. The focus will be on sketching examples of the way that redemption and grace shape the anticipations and expectations which guide the process of inquiry in ethics.

tives of faith and our decisions in situations? This will be the concern of the final section.

## God's Justice (a)

Moral action is action towards the future. In any concrete instance, the future under consideration is usually quite immediate. Most of our action does not envisage the future in terms of civilizations, historical epochs, or ages of the universe. Yet we carry about with us a basic sense of security or anxiety about ourselves and about life in general. It sets something of an atmosphere or backdrop for our concrete deliberations. This sense of security or anxiety is an expectation. It may be an anticipation that we will succeed in our projects. It may be a fear that others will thwart our efforts. It may be a pervasive dread of conflict and a constant worry that we must prepare for battle. Whatever the specific character of our expectations, the fact remains that they are there, they usually perdure through years and decades of our lives and form the way in which we approach our moral deliberations.[97]

These expectations usually have their roots in specific life experiences, often from childhood. The historical origins of our experiences, however, do not limit the scope of their influence in our lives. Generally, our experiences end up shaping our expectations about the whole of life, the whole of the universe, and the whole of what the universe will become. Even when we compare injustices done to us with the success of others, we do not cease to generalize from these limited samples. Our conclusions from such pre-thematic efforts are about the injustice of life, the injustice of the universe. Our expectations make a claim about cosmic order, about ultimate justice.[98]

---

[97] For an excellent analysis which draws upon the work of Lonergan to explore how the Bible shapes our ethical and religious expectations, see Sean McEvenue, *Interpretation and Bible* (Collegeville: Liturgical Press/Michael Glazier, 1994), particularly the essays, "The Bible and Trust in the Future," 65–73; and "The Spiritual Authority of the Bible," 23–39. See also McEvenue, *Interpreting the Pentateuch* (Collegeville: Liturgical Press/Michael Glazier, 1990). The following analysis draws generally upon the works of McEvenue; Gutiérrez, *We Drink from Our Own Wells*; and Eric Voegelin, *The New Science of Politics* (Chicago: University of Chicago Press, 1952).

[98] These terms are used in the sense intended by Voegelin in *The New Science of Politics*. For an excellent discussion of the dynamism of consciousness towards

Ultimately, these expectations make a comprehensive claim. This is because justice is where our pursuit of the good intersects with the path of society and history. When we decide on actions that are subsequently thwarted, we are forced to ask whether we were treated unfairly, or whether our actions warranted the outcome. If we are treated unfairly, we tend to conclude something about the unfairness of life. We may not draw such conclusions explicitly or deliberately, but events still make their contribution to our underlying pre-thematic expectations. Our inner worlds of meaning continue to make their claims on cosmic justice and these claims set the backdrop for our conscious deliberations.

Christian faith challenges us to get in touch with this subterranean world of expectations that shape our conscious moral deliberations. Moreover, faith invites us to name these expectations and critically scrutinize them in the light of the forces of progress, decline and redemption. Faith calls us to cultivate these expectations in a specific direction, a direction that bears upon the question of ultimate justice. Christian faith makes a claim about God's justice. It acknowledges massive structural decline, but does not allow this evil to have the last word. This is because faith is the expectation of the encounter with God's liberating grace in the midst of our experience of sin and evil.

God's justice is not the justice that is realized in our day-to-day achievements of progress; nor is it the sense of justice that has been formed by forces of traumatic decline. Instead, God's justice is revealed most fully in the death and resurrection of Christ, and it continues to be revealed in every encounter with the transformative power of divine love. This is the true justice that pronounces the final word on the justice of the universe. It is a justice that we can expect to encounter throughout life as we open ourselves again and again to grace.

One of the ways this notion of justice forms our moral deliberation is in our attitude towards conflict. Our experiences of conflict and the outcomes of conflict shape our expectations of justice. If we expect to lose in conflicts, we spend our lives avoiding them or building walls

ultimacy in Voegelin's work, see Glenn Hughes, *Mystery and Myth in the Philosophy of Eric Voegelin* (Columbia, MO: University of Missouri Press, 1993). For an introduction to current literature in Christian ethics dealing with the more technical meanings of justice in relation to faith, see John C. Haughey, ed., *The Faith that Does Justice* (New York: Paulist Press, 1977) and David Hollenbach, *Justice, Peace, and Human Rights* (New York: Crossroad, 1988).

to protect ourselves. If we expect to win easily through conflicts, we tend to promote conflict to achieve our goals by prevailing over others. If we experience conflicts as painful, but have learned to do battle to survive, then we spend our lives in constant preparation for battle, and in so doing, we transform all of life into a battlefield.

Faith in God's liberating grace empowers us to face up to conflict and to pursue justice without transforming life into an endless preparation for war. Consequently, faith allows us to build, sustain, and renew social structures, even when they are everywhere threatened by decline. This is not because we underestimate the destructive force of evil, nor is it because we delight in the defeat of the adversary. Rather it is because we trust in God's ability to transform death into life. Faith empowers us to pursue justice in situations of conflict because we expect God's justice to be revealed in the middle of crises, as a power that transcends and heals the cumulative effects of suspicion, mistrust, and despair.[99]

## The Dignity of Persons (b)

One of the most important ways in which Christian faith has shaped ethical deliberation in the twentieth century has been captured in the maxim, "the dignity of persons."[100] In many areas we cannot promote one value without going against another; in health care, in politics, in economic life, in technological research, and in our most intimate relationships, we frequently must promote some values through strategies that contradict other values. One of the tools that Christian leaders have formulated to guide us in our deliberation through such conflicts has been this maxim, "the dignity of persons."

Contrary to what we might expect, this maxim is not rooted in a philosophy of the person, a notion of human rights, or a theory of

---

[99] Avery Dulles provides a fascinating example of how faith shaped the attitudes towards conflict in the early Church in "An Ecclesial Model for Theological Reflection: The Council of Jerusalem," in J. Hug, ed., *Tracing the Spirit* (New York: Paulist Press, 1983) 218–41. See also Donald Bossart, *Creative Conflict in Religious Education and Church Administration* (Birmingham, AL: Religious Education Press, 1980). For a discussion of the way that attitudes towards conflict shape our handling of disputes, see Picard, *Campus Mediation Training Manual.*

[100] For an introduction to current literature on "the dignity of persons," see John Dwyer, "Person, Dignity of," in *The New Dictionary of Catholic Social Thought*, 724–37.

social obligations. It is rooted instead in an understanding of God's redemptive grace. Faith in Christ is faith in God's redemption of all humankind from sin through God's gift of love. This gift is not given selectively to some and not others. It is given to *all* persons. Furthermore, this gift endows all persons with an ultimate destiny, to share in the fullness of this love for all eternity. This eternal union with God is the ultimate destination to which all are called, it is the goal towards which all moral endeavour must strive, and it is the direction towards which grace will always empower us to move. To speak of the dignity of persons is to say that all persons must be treated by other persons with the dignity that God gives them.

Needless to say, we can respond with hosts of questions. Does this mean we must give everyone a vote; a basic income; a VCR? Does it mean we should grant parole to multiple sex offenders? What does it say about the unborn? We could multiply such questions indefinitely. The maxim of the dignity of persons does not "logically entail" answers to any of these questions, but it does rule out a range of attitudes towards society that would treat people as merely cogs in the machinery of world process or as means to some social end. Furthermore, it rules out an attitude that regards persons as irreversibly corrupted by personal or social evil. Grace is a gift to all.

The maxim sets the quest for concrete answers in motion with a distinctive concern, a concern that directs the process of inquiry and gradually yields insights into our moral obligations.[101] It is a concern for all persons as agents of meaning and beneficiaries of God's grace. The maxim requires that *all humans* must be treated as actors, as agents, as participants in the multiple schemes of society and history. This is not because of our actual or potential contributions to the social project. It is because God is at work in the lives of each of us, revealing something of the mystery of salvation history.

---

[101] Chapter 2 of the U.S. Catholic Bishops' document, *Economic Justice for All: Pastoral Letter on Catholic Social Teaching and the U.S. Economy* (Washington: United States Catholic Conference, 1986), is an excellent example of how this maxim, rooted in an understanding of faith, sets the ethical inquiry in motion in a certain direction, guided by specific sets of questions and concerns.

## The Dignity of Persons and the Common Good (c)

Here is where the maxim, "the dignity of persons," begins to connect with our insights into the social structure of moral obligation from Chapter 2.[102] The object of moral deliberation is the common good, understood as a dynamically unfolding ecology of meaning. When viewed from the faith perspective, this ecology will also be subject to the forces of sin, and it will be the place where the mystery of God's redemptive action is being revealed. When one cherishes and nurtures the dignity of persons, one begins to understand the common good not simply as a human obligation and an achievement of human progress, but also as an agent of death and a locus of resurrection.

The elements of social schemes are personal acts of meaning. Hence the common good is not like a machine which is controlled from a central location. Social structures have multiple centres of control. The control which is exercised from the point of each person's input may not be overwhelming or immediately decisive for the overall direction of the scheme, but the role of each person in influencing the course of social schemes is still significant. To speak of the dignity of persons is to recognize that every person has an essential role to play in shaping the course of the common good.

This implies that the common good is fundamentally democratic: it calls for formal democratic institutions. It also requires democracy in a more fundamental sense. We all contribute to social schemes in different ways: through formal channels, when we participate in community, political, or work-related organizations, and also in the day-to-day interactions of our families and work life, as we nurture, sustain, and critique the values and attitudes of social living. Because the common good depends upon the persons who author its constituent events, it must be fully democratic in fostering the hosts of

---

[102] For an introduction to literature dealing with the relation between the person and the common good, see Jacques Maritain, *The Person and the Common Good*; and the essays in Williams and Houck, eds., *The Common Good and U.S. Capitalism*, particularly those by McInerny, Curran, and Novak. See also Hollenbach, "The Common Good Revisited."

institutions and social environments in which citizens deliberate and act to promote good social living.[103]

If the common good demands democracy, it also places obligations on the citizens of democratic societies. The freedom guaranteed by democracies is not without restrictions. These restrictions are obligations that must be met by all citizens. They are not arbitrary, but are rooted in the very structure of democratic social life itself. Because social life is an ecology of social meaning, citizens must discern and accept what is required by the social schemes that are their home. The obligation of persons is to transcend the limitations of self-interest and promote the social structures of the dynamically unfolding common good.

It is not hard to see that the common good will be precarious when virtue is found wanting. Social structures that are open to the input of all are also open to exploitation by anyone who so desires, and ecologies of meaning that make demands on citizens begin to stumble and flounder when citizens fail to live up to these obligations. We can expect these failures to be a regular part of life. The common good is not the Kingdom of God; it is profoundly human and profoundly subject to the forces of sin and decline. If we wish to advance the common good, we must be open to God's saving grace in the personal and social lives of citizens, and supportive of it.

The common good serves the dignity of persons. Therefore social structures that must command our support will be those that build up the dignity of persons and nurture them as responsible agents of social meaning. This process entails liberty and the institutions of democracy, but, more importantly, it entails the religious institutions that nurture faith in redemptive grace.[104]

---

[103] Patrick Byrne and Richard Carroll Keeley provide a fascinating example of this informal dimension to democracy in the work of Jane Jacobs in "LeCorbusier's Finger and Jacobs's Thought: The Loss and Recovery of the Subject in the City," in F. Lawrence, ed., *Communicating a Dangerous Memory* (Atlanta: Scholars Press, 1987) 63–108.

[104] See Robert Doran, "Theological Grounds for a World-Cultural Humanity," in *Creativity and Method*, 105–122.

## The Preferential Option for the Poor ( d ).

A maxim that has appeared more and more frequently in church documents and theological literature in the past two decades, and that tends to cause considerable controversy, is "the preferential option for the poor."[105] This expression, the meaning of which differs considerably from author to author, has been used to justify forms of political action which many Christians find quite troubling. Nonetheless, it remains a significant maxim for our age.

This axiom is an extension of "the dignity of persons." It arises, however, as a distinct guiding principle when we ask what the dignity of the person means in situations where the person seems to have lost all dignity. It asks about dignity when the person lives in crime and poverty, when she is a victim of abuse, when he lives in squalor, when she cannot hold a job, when he is an addict, when she is mentally ill, or when he is a homeless person, a runaway, or a prostitute. The expression was first formulated in the context of liberation theology as Christians from poorer countries of the southern and eastern hemispheres sought a language for their distinctive experiences of God, in situations of grotesque poverty, torture, and political oppression. Since then we have seen that it is relevant to poor, oppressed, and marginalized peoples in our own North Atlantic communities.

The preferential option for the poor is an expression whose meaning, again, is rooted in God's act of saving grace. It means that whenever and wherever people are in need, God's grace is present. The term *the poor* does not refer to a person's annual income. It refers to an experience of need or suffering. In particular, it refers to suffering that happens when people are victims of structures of sin. To say that God shows a "preferential option" does not mean that God likes some people better than others; it means that God's redemptive act of delivering us

---

[105] For an introduction to the debates over the meaning of this maxim, see Donal Dorr, "Poor, Preferential Option for," in *The New Dictionary of Catholic Social Thought,* 755–59; William O'Neill, "No Amnesty for Sorrow: The Privilege of the Poor in Christian Social Ethics," *Theological Studies* 55 (1994): 638–56; Thomas Schubeck, "Ethics and Liberation Theology," *Theological Studies* 56 (1995): 107–122; Patrick H. Byrne, *"Ressentiment* and the Preferential Option for the Poor," *Theological Studies* 54 (1993): 213–41; Stephen Pope, "Proper and Improper Partiality and the Preferential Option for the Poor," *Theological Studies* 54 (1993): 242–71. This analysis draws generally upon Dorr and Pope.

from sin is God's highest and most important activity in history. It is God's "preferred" act.[106]

This theological interpretation is not meant to empty the axiom of its social and political force. In fact, structural sin in our economic and political life is one of the most troubling forms of such sin. Our most common response to people who are poor, outcast, or marginalized, is to view them as second-class citizens. We all do this and we do it so spontaneously that frequently we do not even catch ourselves doing it. This is because our most fundamental moral evaluation of people is done on the basis of our expectations about (moral) progress. We tend to view people spontaneously as contributors to their misfortune. When a person is suffering we often ask ourselves, "What did they do to bring this on themselves?" Just as we hold ourselves accountable for our failings with little regard for the structures that limit our effective freedom, so, too, we often measure others by the same logic of "just desserts." Our most basic tendency is to take outward appearances of progress as the sign of inner worth, and to treat others with dignity only to the extent that we think they have earned it.

God acts differently! God's gift of saving grace is poured out upon all persons, and this gift endows all persons with a dignity we must recognize. For those who are confronted with "the poor," the preferential option for the poor is the moral obligation to recognize this God-given dignity in all who would appear not to have earned it. It is a reminder that the dignity of grace can never be earned, by us or by anyone, and that if anyone claims to have earned God's grace, it must be a false claim. Similarly, the preferential option for the poor reminds us that our spontaneous tendency to judge the moral worth of others by the trappings of progress or success must always be rejected.

For those of us who are victims of sin, poverty, oppression, abuse, or marginalization, the preferential option for the poor is a beacon in the darkness. It reminds us that we are personally chosen to share the most intimate experience of God's infinite love. We can count on God's saving grace because this is the highest and greatest, the most "preferred," of all God's acts. Contrary to all social convention, our lot

---

[106] For a clarification of the theological grounds for speaking of God's "preferential action," see Pope, "Proper and Improper Partiality," 262–64. See also Maritain, *The Person and the Common Good*, 17–20, and particularly note 7.

in life is not a sign of our moral worth, nor should any loss of self-esteem on our part be the last word on our moral capacity. Our dignity, as well as the power to combat sin, is guaranteed by God's grace. Finally, insofar as we have contributed to our own state, our culpability or impotence is never the last word. In our hour of need, we can always know that God has never abandoned us, that God's saving gift to us is always present, that God's redemptive grace always complements our struggles to reverse the structures of poverty and oppression.

## Christian Faith and Moral Deliberation: The Problem of Rules and Contexts

We have been exploring themes that show the impact of Christian faith on moral deliberation. These maxims give rise to a perspective, an attitude, a way of thinking, feeling, and wondering about the events of our moral experience. Yet there remains the challenge of "implementing" these maxims in moral deliberation. What is the relation between these general maxims and concrete moral contexts? To gain some insight into this relation, we must consider a few things about "rules" and "contexts" in moral deliberation.[107]

We work with general moral rules in particular situations or contexts. In everyday parlance we often speak of "applying rules to contexts." The impression given is that we begin with a rule and logically deduce the application from the rule. If we have a rule and want to find out how to implement the rule in a situation, we often think that we must "look inside" the rule to find things implicit in the rule—things that are logically entailed and that tell us in detail how to act in the context. This, however, is not the way things actually work.[108]

---

[107] For a general introduction to the literature and the debates related to rules and contexts, see Richard Gula, *What Are They Saying about Moral Norms?* (New York: Paulist Press, 1982). The classic article on this topic is James Gustafson, "Context Versus Principles: A Misplaced Debate in Christian Ethics," in *Harvard Theological Review* 58 (1965): 171–202. For a discussion of responses, see Richard McCormick, "Current Theology: 1966," in *Notes on Moral Theology 1965 through 1980* (Lanham, MD: University Press of America, 1981) 72–82.

[108] The discussion which follows is my own effort to elaborate upon a host of insights on the role of heuristic structures in scientific inquiry scattered throughout Lonergan's work. See *Understanding and Being*, 63–69, 91–92.

Let us say we have a rule: "Do not lie!" This rule names a class of moral actions, "lies," and is a command or obligation concerning how to behave when considering such actions. In order to understand the rule we need to know something about what makes an action a lie. This is not provided by the rule itself. Instead, the rule presupposes something of this knowledge. Everyday usage of the rule will use a common-sense definition, but this definition may be extremely vague, with little or no indication of how to distinguish between lies and other statements. Indeed, the rule may remain authoritative even when much of this knowledge is lacking. The moment we begin to ask what is entailed in this knowledge, we begin to discover that the technicalities can fill volumes.

There is a core element, unquestionably: a lie involves an untruth. Yet it involves more than this. A mistake can be an untruth and not be a lie. A myth or a novel can involve an untruth and not be a lie. Telling your children about Santa Claus can involve a deliberate, knowing untruth, but it is still not a lie. What, then, defines a lie? We could add that it implies an intent to deceive, but even this is not enough. When we consider untruths told to protect the innocent against unjust and powerful aggressors, we realize that there is an ethical difference between some deliberate untruths that intend to deceive for personal gain and others that intend to deceive in order to protect the innocent. There is an element of injustice in a lie; the intended untruth is not warranted. Someone might respond that we are simply playing with words, but this would be mistaken! We are distinguishing actions that, in fact, are morally different.[109]

Even with all of these subtleties, we have not yet identified all of the elements and skills needed to identify a lie in a particular situation. Even if we have a satisfactory inventory of classes of moral acts we call lies, we still need skills to recognize such particular acts when we come upon them. Lies come clothed in all sorts of garb which frequently make them almost unrecognizable. The task becomes doubly difficult when the deception is well-crafted and supported by conventional authority. To recognize lies often requires skills and virtues to see beyond appearances and to probe beyond the familiar masks of convention or authority.

---

[109] For a recent discussion of literature related to moral differentiation, see John Mahoney, "The Challenge of Moral Distinctions," *Theological Studies* 53 (1992): 663–82.

If you are a young employee, eager to succeed, eager to please, eager to get ahead, you follow the leadership of mentors. You place your trust in them. You must do this if you are to learn your profession. Your mentors tell you a great deal about how to become a professional in your chosen field. They teach you about the technical aspects of your profession, but they also tell you a great deal about the standards of behaviour appropriate to it. In accordance with these standards you may be expected to say things that are untrue, especially in your dealings with clients. Some of these things may be lies, and others may not. To tell the difference requires more than simply knowing the intent of the rule; it requires more than simply listing the differences between this instance and classes of events in this field that are commonly termed lies. It requires that you personally develop the skills needed for seeing beyond the authority or even the virtues of your mentor. The authority of a mentor is a real good. Anyone relying on the authority of a mentor to develop in a profession will have considerable difficulty recognizing a lie when it is clothed in the language of this authority.

This is relevant to our discussion of the role of faith in moral deliberation. To implement a moral rule in a situation, we have to add a host of determinate acts of moral knowing beyond what is entailed in common-sense familiarity with the rule. These acts of moral knowing include differentiating the range of cases to which the rule applies. These differentiations may not have been anticipated in the original common-sense formulation of the rule. These acts of moral knowledge are subsequent acts of moral understanding and judgement that can only be carried out when we wrestle with wider and wider fields of data from human experience. These subsequent acts also call on the virtues and skills required for discerning classes of moral events in different spheres of life.

In a similar way, Christian faith provides a component of central importance to moral deliberation, but, like the moral rule against lying, it needs to be complemented by a range of other components. To provide these other components, we must reach beyond the range of what is logically entailed by the religious rule, gather a host of experiential data, insights, judgements, conceptual differentiations, and skills of discernment, and bring them to bear upon the task of moral deliberation. The final judgement on an action depends, in part, on the component provided by the initial rule, but it also requires all the other components provided by the other operations along the way. Similarly, a batter's determination and commitment say a great deal about the trajectory of a baseball hit into deep left field, but they do not say everything.

The curious and powerful relation between the initial rule and the other elements that come into play in our decision about a lie is surely not a logical relation in the narrow sense. Nonetheless it is a real relation, a *heuristic* relation. What the rule does is guide all of the other operations in the inquiry process in a specific direction.[110] Inquiry is never neutral: it is always directed by concerns and cares, and the concerns expressed by the initial rule lead us as we assemble the other elements. When we make the rule our own, when we make it a guide for our interest, our concern, our search for moral meaning, our quest for how to act rightly, we are set on a path that leads us towards some things and away from others. In our example of lying, we distinguish various elements of the lie because we are interested in promoting the good that lies undermine. If we were driven in our inquiry by a desire to find legal loopholes permitting us to lie with impunity, we would arrive at a very different set of insights, conceptual differentiations, and judgements. Furthermore, concrete discernment would call forth a very different range of habits and skills.

The heuristic force of Christian faith on the other components in the deliberation process is even more striking. This is because faith bears upon our commitment to moral deliberation itself. Faith redresses the tendency to despair over the very value of our operations of moral meaning and action when we are confronted by the intimidating reality of evil. The light of faith does not "logically entail" immediate answers to questions about such things as economic justice, but the commitment of faith animates the operations of the quest for such answers and brings them into play in the process of inquiry.

Moreover, faith brings them into play in a distinctive way. The attitude of joy and gratitude, the forgiveness and reconciliation that flows from the experience of God's love, direct the inquiry in search of specific kinds of solutions to human problems. Where despair counsels desperate or cynical measures, hope invites the exploration of

---

[110] For a similar type of analysis, see Fuchs, "The Absoluteness of Moral Terms," particularly the sub-section, "Norms as Authentic Orientation." See also the general line of analysis in McEvenue, *Interpretation and Bible* and *Interpreting the Pentateuch*.

possibilities for renewing the fabric of human relationships. Neither is logically entailed by the antecedent convictions; the conclusions of each are the final stages of a journey whose initial direction was set by the convictions. Faith is the encounter with grace that renews our relationship with God so that we can pursue the task of renewing our ecologies of meaning. These ecologies, in turn, join us in common action and set the environment for growth towards moral maturity. Christian faith supplies one of the determining components of the final trajectory traced by the moral decision, but this component describes the path along which we assemble all of the others.[111]

## Summary

This chapter has sought to trace some links between Christian faith and moral deliberation on concrete issues. Moral deliberation is not a "logical" matter of deducing implications from first principles, but a process of getting insights and making judgements about concrete moral experiences, guided by Christian faith. It involves distinguishing morally diverse classes of cases, it involves the skills of discerning when and where these classes occur in concrete living, and it involves integrating all of these insights into comprehensive strategies for evaluation and action.

Faith exercises a heuristic force in this inquiry by orienting it in the direction provided by the redemptive encounter with God's grace. There are a number of general attitudinal features to this heuristic force. Faith is joyous and forgiving rather than mean-spirited and vindictive. It is hopeful rather than disparaging and cynical. We considered four theological themes which show this heuristic force of faith in the deliberation process: God's justice, the dignity of persons, the common good, and the preferential option for the poor.

The intention throughout was to illustrate how faith provides a focus of concern in moral deliberation and sets the limits on a range of options that might otherwise appear compelling or appealing. In the realm of justice, faith calls us to get in touch with our personal expectations about ultimate justice and critically assess these

---

[111] Illustrations of this heuristic work of faith are provided by Sebastian Moore in "For a Soteriology of the Existential Subject"; and *Jesus, the Liberator of Desire* (New York: Crossroad, 1989).

expectations, particularly as these relate to the experience of conflicts. Faith proclaims that experiences of injustice are not the last word, and that God's grace will always renew our commitment to justice. Faith does not let the commitment to justice transform history into a perennial battleground. The long-range business of living is building, sustaining, and renewing structures of social living. Finally, God's justice is ultimately a mystery: we can work towards this justice with the confidence that our efforts are always complemented by God's own transformative work of grace, yet our notions of justice are never the whole story.

The notions of the dignity of persons and the common good express some specific directions for reflection on liberty, democracy, and public responsibility. The dignity of persons, grounded in God's saving grace, entails an obligation to treat all persons with a basic respect. It also entails a commitment to democracy at the level of institutions and of family and community life, where the basic values and virtues for democratic living are discussed, evaluated, and reinforced. For the common good, we have to discern and live out our particular commitments to sustain our social living. Finally, the dignity of persons indicates a range of criteria that our social structures must meet, criteria that pertain to the ethical and religious formation of persons.

The preferential option for the poor extends the requirement to respect the dignity of persons to those whose dignity has been lost or violated through oppressive social structures. This is in contrast to our spontaneous inclination to assess a person's worth by the trappings of success. God's redemptive concern for redressing structural sin is God's highest priority, God's "preferential concern," and we must make this priority our own. Finally, for those of us who suffer as victims of structural sin, this theme is a beacon of hope reminding us that, all evidence to the contrary notwithstanding, we have not been abandoned, that we remain the object of God's love and grace.

## Chapter 6

# Where Do We Go From Here?

We are eminently practical people. For the most part, we like to think that our tasks in life are straightforward and that our duty is to get at them and to get them done. Consequently, there is something deeply disturbing about the cacophony of voices that we encounter in our moral world. Disagreement is one thing, but to constantly encounter ever-widening circles of disagreement, not only on the issues, but on the very tools for resolving disagreement, is more than we can handle. It is as if we have been charged with building a house, but have been given access to none of the tools for measuring lengths, laying foundations, cutting lumber, or hammering nails.

These chapters have been dedicated to sketching some of the tools of ethics. Unlike those of carpentry, the tools of moral deliberation are not objects we can hold in our hands. They are tools of meaning, tools of the mind and the heart. Yet, like carpentry, ethics requires the skill, the discipline, and the mastery of the practitioner. The tools of ethics do not produce finished products on their own. They require skill development, and moral skills must be nurtured and cultivated, over long periods and in supportive environments.

We may be practical, but the problems of ethics are not going to be solved in our age by a select team of developers and managers. The task is too large, and the nature of the tools too intimately personal. Effective responses to ethical challenges must enlist the involvement of large numbers of people. Their vision of their task must foster the creativity of vastly diverse individuals and groups, but it must as well be a vision of the *common* good. This is not a problem to be solved once-and-for-all; it is an ongoing project of humanity. Consequently, the challenge of our age is to identify the foundations that can be laid for the labours of future generations. Most significantly, this means renewing our confidence that such foundations do indeed exist, and that the commitment to public moral knowledge and cooperative moral living makes good sense.

I have sought to respond to this foundational challenge throughout these chapters. The effort has been, not simply to introduce the tools of ethics, but to show how we can come to know these tools through attention to the mundane operations of our own daily moral experience. Moral action is not the mechanical application of logical systems or codes; it is a matter of performing operations and skills of meaning. We begin to learn these skills in the first months and years of life, we develop them through years of practice, and we use them daily in meeting the demands of ordinary experience.

At the centre of these chapters there is a core insight. Moral operations and skills involve insights and judgements about schemes of social cooperation. When we speak of actions that are good or right, we are talking about living with other people. Human action always involves some form of participation in the activity of groups. We may have personal interests and goals, but these are seldom realized through our own efforts alone. In understanding how social schemes impose obligations on citizens who would realize their goals through them, we begin to differentiate between good and bad, right and wrong. Furthermore, social schemes themselves never function in isolation; they emerge and flourish or whither and die within the dynamic ecologies of meaning of society and history. As we develop in our understanding of these ecologies, we are furnished with more and more comprehensive tools for evaluating actions, not simply in relation to individual schemes, but in relation to the wider dynamics of historical progress and decline.

Such a vision might lead us to overlook the role of individual persons. The analysis of society as schemes of meaning, however, reveals that there is an integral link between the wide-scale progress of civilization and the intimate life of the person. The conditions of progress are not outside of persons, they are within us, and there is a fundamental condition which must be realized in the intimate lives of citizens for civilization to flourish. The operations of meaning which constitute the schemes of society depend on the liberty and the developed states of virtue of persons. Thus historical progress means foundational obligations which are personal. We must take responsibility for developing character in our own lives and in the lives of others, transcending self-interest, nurturing social order, but also transforming social order towards the longest ranging flourishing of humanity and society.

In reality, we are often indifferent to, or even contemptuous of, the obligations and conditions for self-transcendence. This indifference and contempt can have devastating effects on others, but it can also harness the cooperative structures of history and society to yield social evils which far surpass the devastation wrought by individuals. Our awareness of moral impotence can lead, eventually, to a renunciation of the moral task itself.

Christian faith responds to the reality of structural evil by witnessing to the actions of God. Faith is the testimony to humanity's encounter with the mysterious power of God's grace, working in the midst of evil, reversing decline and extending our own labours towards the good. While grace comes to us from beyond ourselves, it operates within experience, and reveals its fruits to people in the daily events of life. For Christians, the fullest evidence of the reality of this grace is the death and resurrection of Jesus Christ. In praying and celebrating this Paschal Mystery through our lives, Christians cultivate the habits and skills for anticipating and discerning this renewing encounter with grace. While grace is God's work, it renews and informs the direction of our commitment to moral self-transcendence in society and history.

We live in an age which is not sympathetic to the role of religion in public life. Furthermore, we cannot always rely on our religious institutions to provide positive examples. Nevertheless, the religious challenge remains. It is a challenge presented by public opinion, but, most fundamentally, it is a personal challenge. It is we who must wrestle with the challenge of evil. It is we who must confront the problem of despair. While God's gift of grace is continually offered, it is we who must accept it in our lives. In the final analysis, those whose moral lives have been renewed by grace will provide the evidence that will speak loudest in the public realm.

If we are hopeful about the possibility for public reflection on the common good, then we can be joyful in our efforts to promote the common good in our words and in our actions. God's grace not only renews our commitment to social responsibility, it also invites us to work calmly and optimistically towards the achievement of justice. To be sure, this optimism is not naive; it is rooted in the sober recognition of structural evil and the mystery of grace, rather than the expectation of wide-sweeping moral achievement. Still, these are grounds for optimism, and this optimism can be expected to enliven our dealings with those who do not share our views. Frequently, attitudes and ideas change not because we are convinced by others, but because we come to respect them as persons. Then, gradually, we begin to reconsider the ideas that they hold. If there is a primary vehicle of persuasion, it is not our words, but the persons we have become.

Whatever we may think about the social challenges of our age, the fact remains that the course of human history is still in God's hands. We have been given the opportunity to play a role in these events. This role is limited, but it is significant. Our task is to live out our role, wherever we find ourselves. This means understanding and accepting responsibility for ourselves. It means opening our hearts to God. But it is acted out in the daily course of our living with other people.

# Appendix: Study Guide

**Prepared by Paul Allen and Peter Monette**

## Introduction

1. Have you ever experienced yourself as "mysterious" in the way that you make moral decisions? Why is "mysterious" an appropriate term?

2. Think about moral knowing as a set of skills. Can you identify situations in your own life in which moral experiences have involved "skills"? What type of skills were involved? How have you come to possess these skills? What different stages did you go through to perfect these? How were you taught them? What exercises did you have to perform? How are you able to adjust these skills in different contexts?

3. Can you think about an experience in your life in which the distinction between *knowing* the good and *doing* the good was explicit? What did this mean to you at the time?

## Chapter One

1. What is ethics?

2. What are the significant moral sources of your life (religious, persons, authors, ideas, experiences)?

3. What are your values? With whom do you share these values? Who disagrees with these values?

4. Imagine that you are returning merchandise to a large department store. The value of the merchandise is $500. As you are returning the goods, you notice t:.at the clerk has made an error. Instead of crediting your account tl.e proper $500 amount, she credits your account with $1,000. Identify the five moral operations in this example: What is it? Is it so? What am I going to do? Is that action the right thing to do? Are you going to do it?

5. Can you describe your moral horizon? What do you care about, what do you value, what do you not care about or not value? What areas of moral living do you know about but do not understand?

What difference does it make if one's moral horizon does not have a consideration for the "unknown unknown"?

6. Have you ever met someone from a different culture? What was that experience like? What were your feelings about this encounter? Describe the ethical differences and similarities between your two cultures. Did this encounter change you in any way? If so, how? How might the other person be different because he or she encountered you?

7. Can you identify conversion experiences in your life? Contrast your life before a conversion experience with your life afterwards.

8. When do you experience moral disagreement in your life? Describe how this disagreement usually is resolved. How do you go about discussing moral problems with other people? Are you confrontational? Do you avoid conflict? Do you give in to more aggressive people? What do you habitually anticipate when you discover that you disagree morally with another person?

9. To what types of cooperative groups do you belong (family, club, organization, church)? How does belonging to these groups change you? How is belonging meaningful for you? How would your life be different if you didn't belong to these groups? How are other people affected by your involvement with these groups?

10. Describe an experience when you came to someone's assistance. List as many details of this event as you can remember. What were you doing before you knew that the other person needed help? How was your state of being different after you came to help that person? What were your feelings before, during, and after helping the other person? Can you identify the "fact questions" of this event? Can you identify your "action questions"? What values can you identify in this event?

*Glossary*

A **question** is the starting point of the inner drive of human beings searching for moral knowledge. A **question** is the basis for an act that transforms the operation from the internal world to the external, and thereby makes it identifiable by other people.

An **act** is a response to a question that moves someone to operate on the basis of some object, such as moral value. There are five specific acts in moral experience: understanding facts and judging facts (the "fact questions"), understanding values and judging values (the "act" questions), and the decision to act itself.

A **horizon** marks the boundary between that which is known and that which is known simply as unknown (the "known unknown"). Beyond the horizon of that which is unknown lies another, that which marks the difference between the "known unknown" and that which is not even known to be unknown (the "unknown unknown"). Horizons indicate how moral meanings are clustered in relation to each person within his or her time and culture. They become apparent when someone distinguishes between primary and secondary items of importance.

## Chapter Two

1. Imagine that you are having dinner at a restaurant. Identify the different desires that are at play for the people involved (yourself, your dinner guest, the waiter, the manager, and so forth). Identify different stages of the social order that emerge during a meal at a restaurant, describing them in as much detail as you can. What are the different goals for each stage? How does one stage lead to the next? Identify the internal norms (moral obligations) of each stage. What might happen if a particular norm were not satisfied? What function does trust play in this scheme (for example, the fact that a customer pays for the meal only after she is finished, or the fact that the customer does not inspect the restaurant's kitchen prior to eating)? In what way can you say that the various personal desires can only be met through such a cooperative scheme? What larger social structures does this scheme affect? What values are enacted in the scheme (economic, social, personal)?

2. Describe the moral characteristics of drunk driving. What are the contexts? What might be some of the intentions of a drunk driver? What are the larger social structures that are affected by drunk driving? Explain the moral characteristics of drunk driving in terms of the three meanings of the term *good* (personal desire, social order, and value). In what way is a drunk driver's action self-constituting? In what way is it a social act? In what way is the prohibition against drunk driving morally objective knowledge?

3. In what sense is a prisoner both free and not free? Put your explanation in terms of essential and effective freedom.

## Chapter Three

1. Describe in detail a simple conversation that you have had with another person. How were you engaged in role-playing with the other person? In what way were your thoughts, actions, or speech acts influenced by what the other person said or did? In what way were you changed by that other person? Can you identify both "fact" and "act" questions in your conversation?

2. Describe a moral conflict that you have had with another person. What were the issues that motivated the conflict? What were the other person's fact questions? What were yours? What were the other person's value questions? What were yours? In what way were you changed by your participation in this conflict? In what way do you think the other person might have been changed?

3. Identify a particularly difficult moral dilemma in your life. Specify as much detail about this issue as you can. What are your feelings about this? What moral skills do you use to work through this dilemma? Are these skills adequate to the task or do they need refinement? What could you do to make these skills better? Identify the range of both "fact" and "act" questions in relation to the moral dilemma. What sources do you seek out to assist you in working through this moral problem? How are you changed by this moral issue?

## Chapter Four

1. Has your faith, as an aspect of the moral life, animated your moral action? If so, think of one example and identify the ingredients that faith added to this event or situation.

2. Reflect on the Scripture passage that states "There are in the end three things that last: faith, hope and love, and the greatest of these is love" (1 Cor. 13:13). Why are these three things the key to a Christian understanding of morality? How do they relate to one another in structuring moral actions?

3. Can you recall any event in your life where you unintentionally participated in evil through some basic moral incapacity? If so, what did you learn from this event at the time? How would you *develop* this understanding now, given the notions of "horizon," "bias" and the unplanned character of evil that you have just read about?

4. In what sense is there a distinctive Christian ethics, or a particular Christian understanding of responsibility? Try to be specific. How has this distinctiveness played itself out in a story from your own life?

## *Glossary*

**Grace** is the activity of God in the world in order to redeem creation from sin. It is concretely evident in human beings as a gift of the absolutely supernatural. At the same time, it is encountered by us in society and history, especially in the person of Jesus Christ as the one through whom God confronts evil in a climactic event.

**Faith** is knowledge born of religious love. Rather than refusing the challenges which moral experience provides, faith empowers human reasoning in moral knowledge and moral action.

**Evil** is the intended malice of persons and groups as well as the unplanned moral disorder that may not be intended. Structural evil is an indirect result of malice or moral incapacity, but has greater power to accelerate moral failure and discourage people from performing further ethical tasks.

**Chapter Five**

1. Can you identify an event or cluster of events in which you can see the three historical forces (progress, decline and redemption) *actually at work* in the event? Perhaps you can think of an historical event that is widely known to most people. Given that faith is a key dimension to moral experience, can you discern the redeeming quality of the event and the persons in it?

2. Think of a rule or principle that you have followed in your life. What additional insights did you develop in the process of abiding by this principle? Identify the skills and virtue that you cultivated in order to guide this rule in a specific direction. If faith were involved, relate it to the goal that you were trying to achieve. Was that goal relevant to any of the four theological themes discussed in this chapter (divine justice, the dignity of persons, the common good, a preferential option for the poor), and, if so, how?

**Chapter Six**

1. How do you practice the common good? Do you know how you can integrate your personal moral action with a vision of the common good in the region or country where you live? What does this mean in reality? Do you know someone, such as a local community figure or a political leader, who accomplished this well? What is it exactly that makes this person come to mind?

2. Think of a sensitive political or social issue that is meaningful to you. Given what you have read, can you think of ways to commit to this issue personally while ensuring that the goal of social co-operation is sustained? How does God's grace function in your life to renew this commitment to social responsibility? What does witnessing to God's action in the world imply for you? Does it imply being optimistic or not? If yes, what sort of optimism is this?

# Bibliography

## Selected Resources on Ethics in the Work of Bernard Lonergan

### Research Resources

Lonergan Research Institute, 10 St. Mary Street, Suite 500, Toronto, ON, M4Y 1P9, Canada. Telephone: (416) 922-8374; Fax: (416) 921-1673; E-mail: rcroken@chass.utoronto.ca.

Information regarding the *Collected Works of Bernard Lonergan* can be obtained through the Institute. In addition, the Institute maintains an extensive library and a complete, fully indexed catalogue of resources related to Lonergan's work. As a public service to Lonergan scholars, the Institute publishes new entries to the catalogue in the *Lonergan Studies Newsletter*.

The Lonergan Center, Bapst Library, Boston College, Chestnut Hill, MA 02167-3801, U.S.A. (617) 552-8095; Fax: (416) 552-0974; E-mail: croninki@bc.edu. Information regarding *METHOD: Journal of Lonergan Studies*, the activities of the "Lonergan Workshop" at Boston College, and the annual publication, *Lonergan Workshop* (with its numerous supplementary issues), can be obtained through the Center.

The Lonergan World Wide Web site at www.lonergan.on.ca. This site is dedicated to the thought of Bernard Lonergan. It aims to facilitate internet-based collaboration among Lonergan scholars and those interested in Lonergan studies.

The Los Angeles Lonergan Center at Loyola Marymount University, Los Angeles, CA, U.S.A. Web site address: www.concentric.net/~mmorelli. The Center offers links to many Lonergan sites around the world. It also includes information on the Lonergan Philosophical Society and Annual West Coast Methods Conference.

The British Lonergan Association. Web site address: www.appropriate.mcmail.com. The association was founded in 1994 as a network for people in the U.K. interested in the work of Bernard Lonergan.

### Articles and Books

Byrne, Patrick. "Analogical Knowledge of God and the Value of Moral Endeavor." *METHOD: Journal of Lonergan Studies* 11 (1993): 103–35.

_____ . "Consciousness: Levels, Sublations, and the Subject as Subject." *METHOD: Journal of Lonergan Studies* 13 (1995): 131–50.

_____ . "Economic Transformations: The Role of Conversions and Culture in the Transformation of Economics." In *Religion and Culture* edited by T. Fallon and P. B. Riley, 327–48. Albany, N.Y.: State University of New York Press, 1987.

_____ . "Jane Jacobs and the Common Good." In *Ethics in Making a Living*, edited by Fred Lawrence, 169–89. Atlanta, Ga.: Scholars Press, 1989.

_____ . "On Taking Responsibility for the Indeterminate Future." In *Phenomenology and the Understanding of Human Destiny*, edited by S. Skousgaard, 229–38. Lanham, Md.: University Press of America, 1981.

_____ . "*Ressentiment* and the Preferential Option for the Poor." *Theological Studies* 54 (1993): 213–41.

_____ . "The Thomist Sources of Lonergan's Dynamic World View." *The Thomist* 46 (1982): 108–45.

Byrne, Patrick and Keeley, Richard Carroll. "LeCorbusier's Finger and Jacobs's Thought: The Loss and Recovery of the Subject in the City." In *Communicating a Dangerous Memory*, edited by Fred Lawrence, 63–108. Atlanta Ga.: Scholars Press, 1987.

Cassidy, Joseph. "Extending Bernard Lonergan's Ethics." Ph.D. dissertation, Saint Paul University, Ottawa, 1995.

Conn, Walter. *Conscience: Development and Self-Transcendence*. Birmingham, Ala.: Religious Education Press, 1981.

_____ , ed. *Conversion*. New York: Alba House, 1978.

_____ . "Moral Development: Is Conversion Necessary?" In *Creativity and Method*, edited by M. Lamb, 307–24. Milwaukee, Wisc.: Marquette University Press, 1981.

Crowe, Frederick E. "An Expansion of Lonergan's Notion of Value." In *Appropriating the Lonergan Idea*, edited by M. Vertin, 344–59. Washington, D.C.: Catholic University of America Press, 1989.

_____ . "An Exploration of Lonergan's New Notion of Value." In *Appropriating the Lonergan Idea*, edited by M. Vertin, 51–70. Washington, D.C.: Catholic University of America Press, 1989.

Crysdale, Cynthia, ed. *Lonergan and Feminism*. Toronto: University of Toronto Press, 1994.

_____ . "Lonergan and Feminism." *Theological Studies* 53 (1992): 234–56.

_____ . "Revisioning Natural Law." *Theological Studies* 56 (1995): 464–84.

Doorley, Mark. *The Place of the Heart in Lonergan's Ethics*. Lanham, Md.: University Press of America, 1996.

Doran, Robert. *Subject and Psyche*. 2nd ed. Milwaukee, Wisc.: Marquette University Press, 1994.

_____ . *Theology and the Dialectics of History*. Toronto: University of Toronto Press, 1990.

_____ . "Theological Grounds for a World-Cultural Humanity." In *Creativity and Method*, edited by Matthew Lamb, 105–22. Milwaukee, Wisc.: Marquette University Press, 1981.

Fallon, T. and Riley, P. B., eds. *Religion and Culture*. Albany, N.Y.: State University of New York Press, 1987.

Farrell T. and Soukup, S., eds. *Communication and Lonergan*. Kansas City, Mo.: Sheed & Ward, 1993.

Gregson, Vernon, ed. *The Desires of the Human Heart*. New York: Paulist Press, 1988.

Happel, Stephen. "Sacrament: Symbol of Conversion." In *Creativity and Method*, edited by Matthew Lamb, 275–90. Milwaukee, Wisc.: Marquette University Press, 1981.

Happel, Stephen and Walter, James. *Conversion and Discipleship*. Philadelphia, Penn.: Fortress Press, 1986.

Lamb, Matthew, ed. *Creativity and Method*. Milwaukee, Wisc.: Marquette University Press, 1981.

_____ . *Solidarity with Victims*. New York: Crossroad, 1982.

Lawrence, Fred, ed. *Communicating a Dangerous Memory*. Atlanta, Ga.: Scholars Press, 1987.

_____ , ed. *Ethics in Making a Living*. Atlanta, Ga.: Scholars Press, 1989.

_____ . "The Fragility of Consciousness: Lonergan and the Postmodern Concern for the Other." *Theological Studies* 54 (1993): 55–94.

_____ . "The Human Good and Christian Conversation." In *Communication and Lonergan*, edited by T. Farrell and S. Soukup, 248–68. Kansas City, Mo.: Sheed & Ward, 1993.

Loewe, William. "Dialectics of Sin: Lonergan's *Insight* and the Critical Theory of Max Horkheimer." *Anglican Theological Review* 61 (1979): 224–45.

_____ . "Towards a Responsible Contemporary Soteriology." In *Creativity and Method*, edited by Matthew Lamb, 213–228. Milwaukee, Wisc.: Marquette University Press, 1981.

Lonergan, Bernard J. F. *Collection*. Eds. F. E. Crowe and R. Doran. Vol. 4, *The Collected Works of Bernard Lonergan*. Toronto: University of Toronto Press, 1988.

_____ . *Grace and Freedom*. Ed. J. Patout Burns. London: Darton, Longman & Todd, 1971.

_____ . *Insight*. Eds. F. E. Crowe and R. M. Doran. Vol. 3, *The Collected Works of Bernard Lonergan*. Toronto: University of Toronto Press, 1992; orig. 1957.

_____ . *Method in Theology*. New York: Herder & Herder, 1972.

_____ . *Philosophical and Theological Papers 1958–1964*. Eds. R. Croken, F. E. Crowe, and R. M. Doran. Vol. 6, *The Collected Works of Bernard Lonergan*. Toronto: University of Toronto Press, 1996.

_____ . *A Second Collection*. Eds. W. J. F. Ryan and B. Tyrrell. London: Darton, Longman & Todd, 1974.

_____ . *A Third Collection*. Ed. F. E. Crowe. New York: Paulist Press, 1985.

_____ . *Topics in Education*. Eds. R. M. Doran and F. E. Crowe. Vol. 10, *The Collected Works of Bernard Lonergan*. Toronto: University of Toronto Press, 1993.

_____ . *Understanding and Being*. Eds. E. A. Morelli, M. D. Morelli, et al. Vol. 5, *The Collected Works of Bernard Lonergan*. Toronto: University of Toronto Press, 1990.

McEvenue, Sean. *Interpretation and Bible*. Collegeville, Minn.: Liturgical Press/Michael Glazier, 1994.

_____ . *Interpreting the Pentateuch*. Collegeville, Minn.: Liturgical Press/Michael Glazier, 1990.

McShane, Philip. *Economics for Everyone: Das Jus Kapital*. Edmonton, Alberta: Commonwealth Publications, 1996.

_____ . *Lonergan's Challenge to the University and the Economy*. Washington, D.C.: University Press of America, 1980.

_____ . *Process*. Lanham, Md.: University Press of America, 1998.

_____ . *Randomness, Statistics and Emergence*. Dublin: Gill and Macmillan, 1970.

_____ . *Wealth of Self and Wealth of Nations*. Hicksville, N.Y.: Exposition Press, 1975.

Melchin, Kenneth R. "Economies, Ethics, and the Structure of Social Living." *Humanomics* 10 (1994): 21–57.

_____ "Ethics in *Insight*." In *Lonergan Workshop*, vol. 8, edited by Fred Lawrence, 135–47. Atlanta, Ga.: Scholars Press, 1990.

_____ . *History, Ethics and Emergent Probability*. Lanham, Md.: University Press of America, 1987.

_____ . "History, Ethics, and Emergent Probability." In *Lonergan Workshop*, vol. 7, edited by Fred Lawrence, 269–94. Atlanta, Ga.: Scholars Press, 1988.

_____ . "Liberation and Spirituality in Gustavo Gutiérrez." *Pastoral Sciences/ Sciences pastorales* 6 (1987): 65–80.

_____ . "Military and Deterrence Strategy and the 'Dialectic of Community'." In *Religion and Culture*, edited by T. Fallon and P. B. Riley, 293–309. Albany, N.Y.: State University of New York Press, 1987.

_____ . "Moral Decision-Making and the Role of the Moral Question." *METHOD: Journal of Lonergan Studies* 11 (1993): 215–28.

_____ . "Moral Knowledge and the Structure of Cooperative Living." *Theological Studies* 52 (1991): 495–523.

_____ . "Pluralism, Conflict, and the Structure of the Public Good." In *The Promise of Critical Theology*, edited by M. Lalonde, 75–92. Waterloo, Ont.: Wilfrid Laurier University Press, 1995.

_____ . "Revisionists, Deontologists and the Structure of Moral Understanding." *Theological Studies* 51 (1990): 389–416.

Moore, Sebastian. "For a Soteriology of the Existential Subject." In *Creativity and Method*, edited by Matthew Lamb, 229–48. Milwaukee, Wisc.: Marquette University Press, 1981.

_____ . *Jesus, the Liberator of Desire*. New York: Crossroad, 1989.

Price, James. "Typologies and the Cross-Cultural Analysis of Mysticism: A Critique." In *Religion and Culture*, edited by T. Fallon and P. B. Riley, 181–90. Albany, N.Y.: SUNY Press, 1987.

Raymaker, John. "The Theory-Praxis of Social Ethics: The Complementarity Between Hermeneutical and Dialectical Foundations." In *Creativity and Method*, edited by Matthew Lamb, 339–52. Milwaukee, Wisc.: Marquette University Press, 1981.

Roy, Louis and Meissner, W. W. "Toward a Psychology of Grace." *Theological Studies* 57 (1996): 322–37.

Shute, Michael. *The Origins of Lonergan's Notion of the Dialectics of History.* Lanham, Md.: University Press of America, 1993.

Stebbins, J. Michael. *The Divine Initiative: Grace, World-Order, and Human Freedom in the Early Writings of Bernard Lonergan.* Toronto: University of Toronto Press, 1995.

"Symposium: Lonergan's 'Philosophy and the Religious Phenomenon'." *METHOD: Journal of Lonergan Studies* 12 (1994): 121–79.

Tekippe, Terry. *What Is Lonergan Up To in "Insight"?* Collegeville, Minn.: Liturgical Press, 1996.

Vertin, Michael. "Judgements of Value, for the Later Lonergan." *METHOD: Journal of Lonergan Studies* 13 (1995): 221–48.

## Selected Readings on Christian Ethics

Barnes, Jonathan. "Introduction." *The Ethics of Aristotle*, 9–43. Harmondsworth, England: Penguin Books, 1976.

Baum, Gregory. *The Social Imperative.* New York: Paulist Press, 1979.

Beck, Lewis White. "Translator's Introduction." In Immanuel Kant, *Critique of Practical Reason*, vii–ix. Indianapolis, Ind.: Bobbs-Merrill, 1956.

Bellah, Robert, Madsen, Richard, Sullivan, William, Swidler, Ann, and Tipton, Stephen M. *Habits of the Heart.* New York: Harper & Row/ Perennial Library, 1986.

Bossart, Donald. *Creative Conflict in Religious Education and Church Administration.* Birmingham, Ala.: Religious Education Press, 1980.

Browning, Don S. and Fiorenza, Francis Schussler, eds. *Habermas, Modernity, and Public Theology.* New York: Crossroad, 1992.

Childress, James and Macquarrie, John, eds. *The Westminster Dictionary of Christian Ethics.* Philadelphia, Penn.: Westminster Press, 1986.

Christiansen, Drew. "The Common Good and the Politics of Self-Interest: A Catholic Contribution to the Practice of Citizenship." In *Beyond Individualism*, edited by D. Gelpi, 54–84. Notre Dame, Ind.: University of Notre Dame Press, 1989.

Curran, Charles. "The Common Good and Official Catholic Social Teaching." In *The Common Good and U.S. Capitalism,* edited by O. Williams and J. Houck, 111–29. Lanham, Md.: University Press of America, 1987.

Curran, Charles and McCormick, Richard, eds. *Readings in Moral Theology, No. 1: Moral Norms and Catholic Tradition.* New York: Paulist Press, 1979.

Curran, Charles and McCormick, Richard, eds. *Readings in Moral Theology, No. 2: The Distinctiveness of Christian Ethics.* New York: Paulist Press, 1980.

Curran, Charles and McCormick, Richard, eds. *Readings in Moral Theology, No. 5: Official Catholic Social Teaching.* New York: Paulist Press, 1986.

Curran, Charles and McCormick, Richard, eds. *Readings in Moral Theology, No. 7: Natural Law and Theology.* New York: Paulist Press, 1991.

Daly Herman and Cobb, John B., Jr. *For the Common Good.* Boston, Mass.: Beacon Press, 1989.

Davis, Charles. *Theology and Political Society.* Cambridge: Cambridge University Press, 1980.

Desjardins, Joseph. *Environmental Ethics.* Belmont, Cal.: Wadsworth Publishing Company, 1993.

Dorr, Donal. "Poor, Preferential Option for." In *The New Dictionary of Catholic Social Thought,* edited by J. A. Dwyer, 755–59. Collegeville, Minn.: Liturgical Press, 1994.

Dulles, Avery. "An Ecclesial Model for Theological Reflection: The Council of Jerusalem." In *Tracing the Spirit,* edited by J. Hug, 218–41. New York: Paulist Press, 1983.

Dwyer, John. "Person, Dignity of." In *The New Dictionary of Catholic Social Thought,* edited by J. A. Dwyer, 724–37. Collegeville, Minn.: Liturgical Press, 1994.

Dwyer, Judith A., ed. *The New Dictionary of Catholic Social Thought.* Collegeville, Minn.: Liturgical Press, 1994.

Etzioni, Amitai. *The Moral Dimension.* New York: The Free Press, 1989.

Finnis, John. *Fundamentals of Ethics.* Washington, D.C.: Georgetown University Press, 1983.

Fitzgerald, Constance. "Impasse and Dark Night." In *Women's Spirituality,* edited by Joann Wolksi Conn, 287–311. New York: Paulist Press, 1986.

Frankena, William. "McCormick and the Traditional Distinction." In *Doing Evil to Achieve Good,* edited by R. McCormick and P. Ramsey, 145–64. Chicago: Loyola University Press, 1978.

Fuchs, Josef. "The Absoluteness of Moral Terms." In *Readings in Moral Theology. No. 1: Moral Norms and Catholic Tradition,* edited by C. Curran and R. McCormick, 94–137. New York: Paulist Press, 1979.

Gardner, E. Clinton. "New Testament Ethics." In *The Westminster Dictionary of Christian Ethics,* edited by J. Childress and J. Macquarrie, 421–24. Philadelphia, Penn.: Westminster Press, 1986.

Gelpi, Donald, ed. *Beyond Individualism.* Notre Dame, Ind.: University of Notre Dame Press, 1989.

Giddens, Anthony. *New Rules of Sociological Method.* London: Hutchinson, 1976.

Gula, Richard. *Reason Informed by Faith.* New York: Paulist Press, 1989.

_____ . *What Are They Saying About Moral Norms?* New York: Paulist Press, 1982.

Gustafson, James. *Can Ethics Be Christian?* Chicago: University of Chicago Press, 1975.

_____ . "Context Versus Principles: A Misplaced Debate in Christian Ethics." *Harvard Theological Review* 58 (1965): 171–202.

_____ . *Protestant and Roman Catholic Ethics*. Chicago: University of Chicago Press, 1978.

Gutiérrez, Gustavo. *A Theology of Liberation*. Trans. C. Inda and J. Eagleson. Maryknoll, N.Y.: Orbis Press, 1973.

_____ . *We Drink from Our Own Wells*. Trans. M. J. O'Connell. Maryknoll, N.Y.: Orbis Press, 1984.

Haight, Roger. "Jesus and Salvation: An Essay in Interpretation." *Theological Studies* 55 (1994): 225–51.

Hauerwas, Stanley. *A Community of Character*. Notre Dame, Ind.: University of Notre Dame Press, 1981.

Haughey, John C., ed. *The Faith That Does Justice*. New York: Paulist Press, 1977.

Himes, Kenneth. "Social Sin and the Role of the Individual." *Annual of the Society of Christian Ethics* (1986): 183–218.

Hollenbach, David. "Common Good." In *The New Dictionary of Catholic Social Thought*, edited by J. A. Dwyer, 192–97. Collegeville, Minn.: Liturgical Press, 1994.

_____ . "The Common Good Revisited." *Theological Studies* 50 (1989): 70–94.

_____ . *Justice, Peace, and Human Rights*. New York: Crossroad, 1988.

Houlden, J. L. "Jesus, Ethical Teaching of." In *The Westminster Dictionary of Christian Ethics*, edited by J. Childress and J. Macquarrie, 316–20. Philadelphia, Penn.: Westminster Press, 1986.

Hughes, Glen. *Mystery and Myth in the Philosophy of Eric Voegelin*. Columbia, Mo.: University of Missouri Press, 1993.

Jonsen, Albert. "Responsibility." In *The Westminster Dictionary of Christian Ethics*, edited by J. Childress and J. Macquarrie, 545–49. Philadelphia, Penn.: Westminster Press, 1986.

Jonsen, Albert and Toulmin, Stephen. *The Abuse of Casuistry*. Berkeley, Cal.: University of California, 1988.

Jordan, Bill. *The Common Good*. Oxford: Basil Blackwell, 1989.

Keenan, James. "Proposing Cardinal Virtues." *Theological Studies* 56 (1995): 709–29.

_____ . "The Return of Casuistry." *Theological Studies* 57 (1996): 123–39.

Keenan, James and Shannon, Thomas, eds. *The Context of Casuistry*. Washington, D.C.: Georgetown University Press, 1995.

Kerans, Patrick. *Sinful Social Structures*. New York: Paulist Press, 1974.

Lalonde, Marc, ed. *The Promise of Critical Theology*. Waterloo, Ont.: Wilfrid Laurier University Press, 1995.

Langan, John. "Common Good." In *The Westminster Dictionary of Christian Ethics*, edited by J. Childress and J. Macquarrie, 102. Philadelphia, Penn.: Westminster Press, 1986.

MacIntyre, Alasdair. *After Virtue*. 2nd ed. Notre Dame, Ind.: University of Notre Dame Press, 1984.

Mahoney, John. "The Challenge of Moral Distinctions." *Theological Studies* 53 (1992): 663–82.

Maritain, Jacques. *The Person and the Common Good*. Trans. J. J. Fitzgerald. Notre Dame, Ind.: University of Notre Dame Press, 1966; orig. 1947.

McCann, Dennis P. "The Good To Be Pursued in Common." In *The Common Good and U.S. Capitalism*, edited by O. Williams and J. Houck, 158–78. Lanham, Md.: University Press of America, 1987.

McCormick, Richard. "Current Theology: 1966." In *Notes on Moral Theology 1965 through 1980*, 72–82. Lanham, Md.: University Press of America, 1981.

McInerny, Ralph. "The Primacy of the Common Good." In *The Common Good and U.S. Capitalism*, edited by O. Williams and J. Houck, 70–83. Lanham, Md.: University Press of America, 1987.

McInerny, Ralph. *The Question of Christian Ethics*. Washington, D.C.: Catholic University of America Press, 1993.

Mead, George Herbert. *On Social Psychology: Selected Papers*. Ed. Anselm Strauss. Chicago: University of Chicago Press, 1964.

Meeks, Wayne. *The Origins of Christian Morality*. New Haven, Conn.: Yale University Press, 1993.

Melchin, Kenneth R. "National Conference of Catholic Bishops, Canada." In *The New Dictionary of Catholic Social Thought*, edited by J. A. Dwyer, 660–64. Collegeville, Minn.: Liturgical Press, 1994.

Merkle, Judith A. "Sin." In *The New Dictionary of Catholic Social Thought*, edited by J. A. Dwyer, 883–88. Collegeville, Minn.: Liturgical Press, 1994.

Meyer, Ben F. *The Early Christians: Their World Mission and Self-Discovery*. Wilmington, Del.: Michael Glazier, 1986.

Mize, Sandra Yocum. "National Conference of Catholic Bishops, United States." In *The New Dictionary of Catholic Social Thought*, edited by J. A. Dwyer, 665–69. Collegeville, Minn.: Liturgical Press, 1994.

Murray, John Courtney. *We Hold These Truths*. Kansas City, Mo.: Sheed & Ward, 1988; orig. 1960.

Noonan, John T., Jr. *Contraception*, enlarged ed. Cambridge, Mass.: Harvard University Press, 1986; orig. 1965.

_____ . "Development in Moral Doctrine." *Theological Studies* 54 (1993): 662–77.

_____ . *The Scholastic Analysis of Usury*. Cambridge, Mass.: Harvard University Press, 1957.

Novak, Michael. "Free Persons and the Common Good." In *The Common Good and U.S. Capitalism*, edited by O. Williams and J. Houck, 222–43. Lanham, Md.: University Press of America, 1987.

O'Connell, Timothy. *Principles for a Catholic Morality*. Rev. ed. San Francisco: Harper & Row, 1990.

O'Keefe, Mark. *What Are They Saying about Social Sin?* New York: Paulist Press, 1990.

O'Neill, William. "No Amnesty for Sorrow: The Privilege of the Poor in Christian Social Ethics." *Theological Studies* 55 (1994): 638–56.

Pirsig, Robert M. *Zen and the Art of Motorcycle Maintenance: An Inquiry into Values.* Toronto/New York: Bantam Books, 1974.

Polanyi, Karl, Arensberg, Conrad M., and Pearson, Harry W., eds. *Trade and Market in the Early Empires.* Chicago: Henry Regnery Company/Gateway Ed., 1971; orig. 1957.

Pope, Stephen. "Proper and Improper Partiality and the Preferential Option for the Poor." *Theological Studies* 54 (1993): 242–71.

Rawls, John. *A Theory of Justice.* Cambridge, Mass.: Harvard University Press, 1971.

Ricoeur, Paul. *Oneself As Another.* Trans. K. Blamey. Chicago: University of Chicago Press, 1992.

Schnackenburg, Rudolf. *The Moral Teaching of the New Testament.* Trans. J. Holland-Smith and W. J. O'Hara. New York: Herder and Herder, 1965.

Schubeck, Thomas. "Ethics and Liberation Theology." *Theological Studies* 56 (1995): 107–22.

Schuck, Michael. "Modern Catholic Social Thought." In *The New Dictionary of Catholic Social Thought,* edited by J. A. Dwyer, 611–32. Collegeville, Minn.: Liturgical Press, 1994.

Smart, Ninian. "Relativism in Ethics." In *The Westminster Dictionary of Christian Ethics,* edited by J. Childress and J. Macquarrie, 531–32. Philadelphia, Penn.: Westminster Press, 1986.

Spohn, William. "Jesus and Christian Ethics." *Theological Studies* 56 (1995): 92–107.

—————. "The Return of Virtue Ethics." *Theological Studies* 53 (1992): 60–74.

Stevens, Edward. *Business Ethics.* New York: Paulist Press, 1979.

United States Catholic Conference. *Economic Justice for All: Pastoral Letter on Catholic Social Teaching and the U.S. Economy.* Washington, D.C.: United States Catholic Conference, 1986.

Vaney, Neil. "Evil, Social." In *The New Dictionary of Catholic Social Thought,* edited by J. A. Dwyer, 366–69. Collegeville, Minn.: Liturgical Press, 1994.

Voegelin, Eric. *The New Science of Politics.* Chicago: University of Chicago Press, 1952.

Walter, James J. "Christian Ethics: Distinctive and Specific?" In *Readings in Moral Theology, No. 2: The Distinctiveness of Christian Ethics,* edited by C. Curran and R. McCormick, 90–110. New York: Paulist Press, 1980.

Walzer, Michael. *Spheres of Justice.* New York: Basic Books, 1983.

Whitney, Barry L. *What Are They Saying about God and Evil?* New York: Paulist Press, 1989.

Williams, Oliver, and Houck, John, eds. *The Common Good and U.S. Capitalism.* Lanham, Md.: University Press of America, 1987.

Winter, Gibson. *Elements for a Social Ethic.* New York: Macmillan, 1966.

# Author Index

# Subject Index

## A

Acts.
*See* Questioning, concerning acts

Authenticity, 13, 65–66, 67, 99

Authority, 20–21, 106, 118, 119

## B

Bias, 91–93, 100, 103, 108

## C

Capacities, moral, 14, 34, 47, 65, 66, 67, 68, 69, 71, 74, 78, 80, 90–91, 92, 93, 96, 97, 99, 102, 105, 117

Care. *See* Horizons, moral

Casuistry, 62, 118

Character, moral action and, 20, 66–68, 69, 72, 75, 124

Christ, 9, 88, 98, 99–101, 112
death and resurrection of, 101, 110, 125

Christian faith
democracy and, 113, 114, 123
ethics and, 8–9, 14, 88–90, 97–99, 104–5, 107–22, 125
heuristic function of, 14, 120–22
hope and, 97–98, 120–21
moral deliberation and, 107–22, 125

Commitment, role in contracts, 51–52

Common good, the, 10–11, 123, 125
dignity of persons and, 113–16, 122
social structures and, 11, 113, 122

Consequences, 39–40, 42, 51, 71–72, 97–98

Contexts, 39–40, 53, 54, 66, 75
principles and, 108–9, 117–21

Contracts
commitment and, 51–52
social structures and, 49

Conversion
moral, 30–31, 34
religious, 30
*See also* Transformation

Cooperation, 44, 46, 51, 53, 78, 93, 105, 107, 124, 125

## D

Decision, 4, 6, 7, 12, 26–27, 34, 47, 48, 52, 65, 66, 68, 69, 75, 76, 77, 78, 98, 120, 121

Decline, progress and, 40, 41, 43, 56, 77, 79–80, 102–4, 107–8, 110, 124

Deliberation, 4, 5, 6, 9, 19, 43, 44–45, 47, 59, 75, 81, 92, 96, 98, 107–22, 123

Democracy, ethics and, 1, 9, 75–76, 113–14, 122

Desires, 46, 47, 54–57
levels of moral meaning and, 43–44, 80

Despair, 95–97
hope and, 125

Development, moral, 7–8, 47, 67–68, 75, 76, 78, 79, 90, 100, 124

Dignity of persons, 111–15, 116, 122

Direction of change, 37–39, 45–46, 104, 121

Discourse scheme, 50, 54, 71, 72, 119

Dynamism, moral, 17–20, 19, 21, 33, 97, 98

## E

Ethics
Christian faith and, 8–9, 14, 88–90, 97–99, 104–5, 107–22, 125
democracy and, 1, 9, 75–76, 113–14, 122
morality and, 6
New Testament and, 99–102
religion and, 4–5, 82, 87–89, 95–97, 99, 125